Football For Life

Simon Cooper

authorHOUSE®

AuthorHouse™ UK Ltd.
500 Avebury Boulevard
Central Milton Keynes, MK9 2BE
www.authorhouse.co.uk
Phone: 08001974150

First published by AuthorHouse 12/17/2009

ISBN: 978-1-4490-5801-2 (sc)

This book is printed on acid-free paper.

*"Greater love hath no man than this,
That a man lay down his life
for his friends."*

ST JOHN 15:13

"Do It"

Spencer W. Kimball

"Dreamers achieve the impossible dreams"

Mike Taylor

"Live by the sword, die by the sword"

Christopher Moynahan

"A great teacher is one who listens"

Harry Cooper

INTRODUCTION

"Mandy, I don't feel right"........ My breathing wasn't right....

"I want to go to the hospital now....Mandy" I was panicking.

Mandy rushed in the room from upstairs,

"What's wrong, what's wrong?"

Her expression looked worried as she took one look at my face and knew it was serious.

"I can't breath properly, I'm really struggling breathing"

I was worried, real worried, Mandy had just had our second daughter Millie Rose, she was only four months old, 6 weeks after she was born Mandy had lost both her parents Rose & Gordon, she had been through so much pain and grief that I just didn't want to add to it.

"Shall I phone an ambulance?"

I looked at Mandy's face and from it I could read everything she was thinking.

I've never been scared of dying as I believe in life after death, but since I've had my own family I am scared, because I don't want to leave this earth till I've done my job of being a father to my kids.

I couldn't even speak so I just did the steering wheel motion with my hands and stood up. I remember being sat in the passenger seat, leaning my head against the window and looking at the lawns of our neighbours and proper taking everything in on our cul-de-sac on Coronation Road. Something inside me was saying that I might not be coming back. I was praying to God in my head not to take me yet as it wasn't fair on Mandy as she couldn't possible lose 3 people in her family in such a short space of time but inside I knew that God did things for a reason and very rarely did deals.

We arrived at Royal Oldham Hospital and walked straight into Accident and Emergency. As soon as Mandy explained I had breathing difficulties I was on a mobile bed with a curtain being drawn round me,

 "I love you"... Mandy said, as she held my hand,

"I love you too" I replied.

I could see tears forming in her eyes; I was now screaming a prayer in my head to God telling him he was out of order if he were to let me die now. I'd done some wrong things in my time but Mandy had been a saint all her life and she had just lost her mum and dad, losing her partner now would just be too much for her to go through.

All of a sudden I'm having the curtain pulled around me, nurses putting wires on me, and a doctor putting plasma in my arm, "He's having a heart attack" What?? I thought in my head!

I wasn't having a Heart attack! I was 32 years old, I'd seen heart attacks on television, and they didn't look like this!! But hey they're the professionals and who was I to argue?

The nurses usher Mandy out of the area and I can hear her crying, confused and asking will I be ok. Oxygen mask goes on; their whacking plasma up my arm and it's all too much for me to take in. The weird thing was I didn't feel like I was having a heart attack, but all the panic was making me panic. I remember a fat female nurse bending over and picking something up off the floor, I was thinking to myself the last thing I'm going to see in my life is a size 18 arse in navy blue pants!

All of a sudden a senior doctor rushes in and takes a look at my results again on the heart scanner, has a feel of my head and tells the nurses and junior doctor something, and everyone disappears except one nurse,

"Bit of a false alarm Simon, Dr Smith raised a bit of a false alarm, but Dr Zaid has said your scan had just picked up a tiny clot in your blood stream and it's nothing to worry about"

At no time in my life was I happier to hear an Oldham Accent from a nurse with a size 18 arse! I just put my head back in the pillow and carried on floating on the oxygen, Mandy came back in and put her arms round me and kissed me,

"I thought I'd lost you, I really did".. We both cried - with relief more than anything.

They kept me in Royal Oldham for 5 days and I had every scan and test for cardiology you can think of. They finally came to the conclusion that I had an infection around the muscles near my heart. I was later to find out it was through an infection of a rotten wisdom tooth that I had not gone to the dentist with. Your wisdom teeth are connected to your heart by blood vessels and are very dangerous if not addressed when they decay. This causes Endocarditis which is a rare condition which causes inflammation of the heart lining, heart muscles and heart valves. Although relatively uncommon, endocarditis is a serious and potentially fatal condition. However, with the appropriate treatment and care, most people with Endocarditis recover.

As you can see, I did read up on my condition and its pretty frightening stuff. Whilst they were doing the scans the doctors also informed me that I had a leaking Aortic valve. They said that this was quite common (I later found out from my mum that both my grans had leaking valves) and it was something I would have to have regular checkups on every 4 or 5 years.

One thing that did my head in was that every day I was being told I could go home tomorrow, only for the doctors to change their minds the following day. I felt brand new after 2 days and was getting depressed as I wanted to get out of the place and City were in Europe for the first time in decades in a couple of days and I was running a coach!

I used to watch people on the ward who had suffered major heart attacks, just staring into thin air, thinking and repenting in their heads as I had done before I had received my diagnosis. The place had a cold feeling to it and I wanted out as soon as possible. I remember being in bed one night, I was half asleep and I saw in the corner of my eye one of the patient's silhouettes creeping over to my bed. I jumped up!

"Come near me and I'll break your neck mate"

I thought he was going to try and have a dabble with me while I was asleep and he just put his finger on his lip and went "sssssssssshhhh"

"Never mind sssssssssshh what do you think you're doing knob head?"

"Would you like a sip of nectar" He stunk of booze and held a small bottle of whiskey up to my head.

"Are you not right in the head mate or what? Do one now before I put it over your flipping head."

I still wasn't sure whether he was a shirt lifter or not but was taking no chances by having a drink with him at two in the morning on a hospital ward. The fuss woke half the ward up, and the night nurse came over and went ballistic at him. The nurses and doctors were fantastic in there, and one in particular was a local woman called Pat Rule from Failsworth. As I was a Failsworth lad she looked after me and I was really grateful to her as she was constantly reassuring me I would be ok, and made me realise I was lucky compared to some of the other patients.

People go on about all the foreign doctors in this country, well let me tell you they are all fantastic and no matter what your opinions on immigration or race are no one has the right to judge a person over his skin colour, and I just wish everyone had the experience of having a foreign doctor being in control of their life. I actually got talking to a Persian heart surgeon once who was wearing a black eye, I asked in jest had his wife cracked him, he told me that a mixed race lad and two white lads just attacked him in the street for no reason whatsoever. They said nothing at all and just left him on the floor in Salford Precinct in the daytime, I was shocked to hear it had happened to him four times while he had been in England. I asked him what he would do if he ever had them on an operating table in front of him. He just looked at me smiled and said,

"Mr Cooper, I fix hearts and am a sort of plumber like you, I sadly cannot fix sick minds, but I would give the patient the best treatment I possibly could and pray with gods help the mind sickness resolves itself over time. It's a very powerful thing the power of forgiveness"

Those words made me think back to my youth when I was a teenager giving abuse with many others to anyone who was Asian or looked a bit foreign in my area. I had changed as I got older and became more multi-racial especially meeting lads at the match who were black or Caribbean. Many of them became my best mates and over a short space of time I realised it was just ignorance that was making me judge people for the colour of their skin or their dress code.

I was not a racist kid due to my mum's religious teachings, but in the area where I was brought up people were scared of mixing as the area was mostly white and anything different was seen as a threat.

The doctor's words though hammered it home to me then that I was the last person to judge another person, especially over the colour of their skin or their dress sense. For all I know one of those people I abused could have been this surgeon's relative, yet here I was on a slab with him prepared to save my life if I needed him to.

While I was in hospital my first non-family visit was off two reds called Peter Ravenscroft and Stephen Scullion who are now great friends and things like that I just don't forget. As I said, I was itching to get out and one of the main reasons was City were playing in Europe and I had organised a coach with a couple of friends... Spike Merricroft, Chris Dryer and Peter Trant. It was to drive all the way to Belgium to watch City play Lokeren in our first European football for years, and passengers were panicking and some even thought I was dead! Luckily two good friends Dryer and Tranter from Blackley sorted everything out but I missed them setting off and was gutted.

Spike had phoned Mandy and told her if I got out the day before the game he had a spare plane ticket and I could go to Belgium with his chartered plane. As soon as Mandy informed me of the news I was asking Pat the nurse to word the doctors up that I was going to sign myself out if they didn't let me out, City were in Europe and there was nothing that was going to stop me going to the game. Mandy was more than unhappy but knew her argument would not even have a case.

The morning before the day of the game I woke up in bed in the hospital with 4 doctors looking at me...

"Right Mr Cooper, you can go home today, but you must rest and take it easy. We're giving you two courses of antibiotics that you MUST take and we will see you in 2 weeks. Oh and by the way....... no flying, it could be risky"

In my head I was replying..."No flying...you're having a laugh, I'm sweet mate and City might not be in Europe ever again so I will take my chances!"

I just nodded but I was already packing as soon as he said "today" and after saying goodbye to all the nurses I got Mandy to pick me up and I was gone.

When you think you're going to die its true what they say about you seeing your life flashing before you....When I saw mine it was full of football!

This story is about how my life has evolved around the game, from following the team I support to the teams I've managed and even played in at school. The characters I have met, and the paths in life it has led me down. How I was persecuted as a child for my families Christian beliefs and how the feeling of not being accepted made me rebel towards society and look for a way to blow off my anger by becoming a football casual.

I also share how the amateur game substituted my passion for the Premier League for a lot less money and a lot less trouble and gave me greater personal achievements, as well as making my family more secure.

I share a few experiences of being part of Manchester City's Young Guvnor Hooligan element from their start in 1988 to the millennium. Many of them became great personal friends and many still are. All of them I love like brothers which may be hard to swallow for the average reader, but over the course of my story many of you will understand why. The story won't be stating who done who, where, when, and why...because that was not what it was about in my eyes. It was about the rush, the friendship, the trust and the camaraderie between a bunch of lads from all different walks of life who travelled all over the country having the funniest and best times of their lives from the late 80's right through the Madchester rave scene, to the new millennium.

It would be wrong of me to condone or criticise football gangs, as I would contradict myself on both sides of the fence. Reading this book will share with you my feelings on that subject as well as many others. A major input in this book and in changing my life was the role of playing and being involved in amateur football. From playing (which I was no Dennis Law) to managing (which I was pretty good at) I will show you the other side of the game that re-kindled my love of the game after part of me died a little, with the death of Maine Road and the lack of football pitches locally for kids teams in Manchester's grassroots football.

Instead of fighting off the pitch against opposing fans I changed my ways to fight off the amateur pitch for more pitches and better kid's football facilities with local councils and the F.A. Also how mistreatment of fans by the club I loved led me into getting involved with supporters groups such as Safestanding.co.uk, The Fans Committee at Manchester City, Atmosphere Action Group and creating Bluewatchmcfc, an independent supporters group.

How a new regime in the City Boardroom led myself and others to become that upset with football that we became involved in an unsuccessful group of City fans that thought of breaking away from the club and re-forming it as a "fans club"..... Blueprinting Man United's breakaway club F.C United. When the book breaks it down and goes deep into the thought of that venture, it may start ringing a few bells in your head and chords in your heart.

I still believe to this day that one day F.C United will become the saviour of Manchester United as we know it. Don't get me wrong I hate MUFC as much as the next blue, but I have always had an understanding of the reasons why 5000 hardcore United fans would breakaway and re-form their own club. The reasons for that will open up to you in the book and you may relate them to your own club. For people involved in amateur football, whether it is you or your kids I will try and expose the bad management of the game in this country and the rot that is set in, that will most definately bring repercussions to the national game

The story also talks about my addiction for over 12 years with cocaine and how it slowly dragged me down to the depths of hell. Without a shadow of a doubt writing this book and telling this story has changed my life and helped cure my addictions and it's something I want to share. I also want to share my story on how I returned to attending church after 21 years of denying the knowledge I was taught as a child. How my Christian religious beliefs helped me cure my addictions and look at the game in a different way.

All in all I just want you, the reader to enjoy the book and most of all be able to relate to it. Hopefully it may just have an input in your life and have a positive input in the game. It's not the most well structured book as I am no Enid Blyton or scholar of literature, I am just passionate about the game and want to express my feelings on the subject Most of all though I want you to feel the soul of the game that I am trying to share and I pray it gives as much joy to you and your family's life, as it has to me and mine. Hopefully though, you'll choose a few wiser paths than me!

Every word is the truth and I don't believe the foundation of any good book could be any different. There might be a few mistakes with dates, name and places but I even though the reader may not relate to the characters I know you will relate to the circumstances.

People will say who am I to write a book? Me.............. I'm just an average Mancunian lad from a one parent family now with a so called 'dysfunctional' family, who was a prankster at school. I am a proud 37 year old granddad to Brodie Hurst. I work as a Surveyor who earns £300 to £400 a week. No mega qualifications, terrible at washing the pots and always farting like all good dads do!

The word "Life" is also in the book title and in conjunction with football I have written about what I have learnt in my life whilst involved in football and related subjects that affect us all as human beings living in the same society.

I have declined from changing anything as I look upon it as though I would be trying to hide who I was and who I am now and that is not how I wish to be portrayed. I just want it to come across as the truth, which it is.

Why do I want to write a book? Well a few friends who I have watched struggle with life have inspired me. I have learnt to be grateful for what I've got and always aspire to learn more in life every day I breathe. If this book is a failure or a success at least I can look back and say to myself I had a go.

Proceeds from this book will be going to The British Heart Foundation and a charity which supports sufferers of Multiple Sclerosis in respect of a good friend of mine Anthony Rowan from Fallowfield. Also I will hopefully be able to donate proceeds to a few local grassroots football teams which are close to my heart.

When I first started writing this book I was a totally different person to the one I am now finishing it and I hope you can see that in the way it comes across. It has taken me nearly two years to publish and it has been the hardest challenge I have ever come across in my life. During the process I have lost two great friends and it has affected me deeply and made me more humble.

What's the moral of the book? People can change for the better, and football is a great tool to help society to achieve this...... It just requires faith and belief. Maybe I use the word "I" too many times, but deep inside I know if you relate to the book you can replace that word with "We" in your mind.

CHAPTER ONE

"KICK IT BACK TO ME SON"

Chapter tunes
The Beat - Can't get used to loosing you
The Clash - Jimmy Jazz
Pink Floyd - Mother

If we all think back to our earliest memory of how we were introduced to football, nine times out of ten it's with your friends or family, most probably your dad taking to you to the park to see if you had "the gift".

I was no different to any other son, nor was our kid Louis. I remember it to this day, my dad taking us to a field in Agecroft in Salford with a bright orange Mitre football. As we got out of the car he would run a few yards and think he was Dennis Tueart, I remember him showing us how to kick the ball with the inside of your foot, "this is called a pass" he would say!

At the time we found the dog funnier, as it would chase the ball every time my old fella tried kicking it to us. Our kid and me would be in hysterics as he would chase the dog dribbling the ball with its nose all around the field. (It was a Jack Russell) So due to this, our dads coaching sessions didn't last very long and the rest of our football education came from the schoolyard. In the infants' school it was rare someone brought in a full size football so most of the time we played with a tennis ball with no nets. It was just a pack of kids trying to dribble round the yard, the ones who were crap just whacked it as hard as they could and everyone made chase.

Around this time I remember an assembly being called as our school, Mather Street Primary had won the junior league in the local area. I remember being sat there as they were applauded in, dressed in the full navy blue kit with smiles like Cheshire cats. Every one of them was a hero and a legend in school and it is what every lad including myself wanted to emulate playing football.

When we moved up from infant school to junior school the first thing we noticed was that playtimes just involved pure football. The schoolyard was set out the ideal size for an enclosed football pitch with a fence down one side and the school windows on the other. At the goal ends you had a big red brick shed with a slate roof, and the other goal was created by an enclosure for the bins and waste food from the kitchens to create car access for the yard. It was perfect for non-stop football, as it never went out for a throw-in unless we had a crap goalkeeper who could not kick.

To top it off, ours was the first year that the headmaster had decided to divide the yards into male and female yards. So our yard was all male, this made play time football time! 60 young kids, 30 a side, one ball, no ref and no rules, just the PE teacher looking on from a window for potential players for the school team. Some days it would be City v United, other days it would be picked teams, 1st years were always picked last therefore we were always last!

Within my first year I had learned in that schoolyard how to distribute the ball quickly, whether it be passing or shooting. If you didn't you would get clobbered off a 4th year player and taken out. This carried on out of school as on our street we had an array of football talent that were all older than our Louis and me. You all as readers will have your own mentors but on our street it was Jimmy Ford, Mickey Ford, Johnny Mac, Chris Lamb, and Andrew

Lamb. They were all older lads that we played with for hours at the side of Pifco Mill in Failsworth. Some games in the 6 week school holidays were played for up to 8 hours with breaks only allowed if someone's parents turned up with "jublee's" or a bag of ice pops. A Casey (leather football) would not last a full day due to wear and tear, and flyaway's (cheap balls) would pop.

We literally played till the ball was worn out or popped, then go home and watch Kick off with Elton Welsby on a Friday, or Saint and Greavsie and Match of the Day on a Saturday. We became football mad!

At about this time my mum and dad got divorced, and this had a major impact on my life, I started to become a rebel and was getting in trouble a lot in and out of school. I was getting involved in car crime as well as burglary of commercial premises that were mainly all the local mills in Failsworth. Also other less serious things like annoying neighbours by collecting dog pooh in old newspapers, placing it on a doorstep, lighting it and running away hiding. The neighbour would come out of his house and stamp the fire out caking his shoe and pants in pure dog pooh...happy days. Or tying cotton to people's door knockers and pulling it from 10 metres away hidden behind bushes or a car, then watching the neighbours be baffled with no one being at the door. We would do this till it haunted them!

Due to all the trouble I was bringing to our home, my mum decided in her great wisdom to get us a black and white portable TV for our room to keep us in the house more. This was a dream and no one on our street had one.

As my mum always watched Coronation Street over the years me and our kid would watch Villa, Forest, Liverpool, Ipswich and Everton have European success with all the kids off the street watching live European midweek matches in our bedroom. Yes every one had a TV but we just all loved watching it together on the box in our bedroom, then replaying it ourselves in our heads in the school yard the next day.

At the weekend my mum and dad agreed through the courts that we could spend Saturdays with my dad. He started taking us to

Maine Road to watch City, at first it was a bit frightening as in the late 70's City were doing well with Tony Book as manager and the ground was hammered every week which was a bit daunting for a lad of 6 years old and his 5 year old brother.

My dad was a bus driver, and at that time if you were a City fan from the north side of Manchester you got a bus from Aytoun Street next to the Britannia Hotel in the city centre which took you to the game. All the bus drivers were given free access to the game and congregated at the back of the old wooden Platt Lane.

I remember it was a game against Spurs in the 76/77 season, and I wasn't really interested in the game as I was just astonished at the amount of people all in one place, the noise, the smells, the faces, the songs, the swearing, the conversations and the fact that Dennis Tueart, our hero was somewhere on the pitch. It was just too much for me to take in, and I was in the zone, just dumbstruck! I wouldn't say at that time it was enjoyable, it was just a new adventure with my dad and I was happy just to be with him. Not having my dad there Monday to Friday I used to miss him and I knew our big connection was football and I missed his coaching sessions.

The City thing hadn't really kicked in with me yet, but I was slowly coming round to it. I remember to this day when that happened. It was that game...Spurs..............

City scored and my dad grabbed both our Louis and me and swung us around like rag dolls, I remember seeing the joy on his face and all the other fans around us. The noise was like nothing I had ever heard before; it grabbed the inside of my stomach and wrapped it around my heart so I could feel it beating. It was something I was to become addicted to, and still am. Our kid and me just looked at each other, smiled and hugged our dad, we had found something that connected us all and brought us all joy - It was football!

I remember the second and third goals went in and we were over our dad before he could even celebrate. We were now that confident, we were joining in the singing with the rest of the Platt Lane... "CITY WE LOVE YOU, WE LOVE YOU CITY WE DO...OHHH CITY

WE LOVE YOU" The game ended up with Booth, Tueart, Barnes, Hartford and Kidd scoring and City winning   5-0. It was heaven!

Things that stick in my mind about that first game was the togetherness of everyone inside that ground. It didn't matter how old you were, how you looked, dressed or even where you came from. If you were in the City end you were accepted, it was one big happily family with one thing in common Manchester City F.C The blues were now my family, our Louis' family and my dad's family, we were all connected with everyone in that ground and it was great to be a part of that.

Afterwards I remember having to always leave early and my dad would have to start the bus on Lloyd Street near the Parkside pub waiting to take the City fans back to the city centre. He would then return the bus to the Queens road depot and take us back to his house in Salford with a pink final that our kid and me would fight for. The pink was a sports paper that had all the days match reports in and every stat you would want.   After reading that for an hour or so, me and our kid would get out Subbuteo, which was the 70's and 80's equivalent of your Playstations FIFA game in the modern day.   It was a felt pitch laid out on the floor with two teams of little figures of men with a half ball attached to their feet. When we played it was major pride at stake, and many a time we would have to glue the men back together because one of us had smashed a full team of these little figures up the previous week through having a rage at losing.

We also collected Panini stickers and football cards that came with a free chewing gum stick with every pack.. Every kid at school collected these and it was a major currency that got you by in junior school. Games were played such as "Topsys" in which two players stood 5 cards each against the wall, each player then had to throw other cards at the wall cards and knock them down, whoever took the last card down won whatever was on the floor. At one point our kid and me had a two-foot tall pile of cards we had collected and won at school. Panini sticker albums must have cost parents a fortune, and I remember being king for a day when our mate Andrew Lamb robbed a full box from Ivells the newsagents on Oldham Road. We ate that much chewing gum our jaws ached for days.

Football in the late 70's and early 80's was what every male did in Manchester. If you weren't watching you were playing. With no shops or pubs open on a Sunday afternoon, amateur football was huge. I remember watching games on Lord Lane and at the back of Stansfield Road School after sneaking out before my mum took us to church. I was mystified why people punched each other's heads in over a game, it was something that I would see more of as I grew up!

As my mum brought us up as a strong Christian family (Mormons) she installed non-violent morals and standards within our house. I found this very difficult over the years, as other kids would see that I would never hit back and was a bit timid. I knew my capabilities as I was a big lad for my age but I had the fear of sin installed in me and was told that I was carrying the name of Christ being a latter day saint.

Sometimes though I would just blow a fuse and when I did I just totally lost the plot big time. It was like all the punches I soaked up over the years would just build up inside me and I would lose the plot big time. Sadly a lot of the time my younger brother was on the receiving end, although the first time I proper lost it was defending him.

There was a huge lad and friend of ours called Neil McKelvie who lived on the next street. For some reason I remember him dragging our Louis on the floor and I just flew into him like a Tasmanian devil. Neil just focussed his attention to me and just slapped me all over but I remember I just felt no physical pain as my head was raging and it was not registering with my body. It scared me after as the only time I remember stopping was when a few of the older lads grabbed me and calmed me down. think this stems from a time I was collecting firewood with a huge group of us from Failsworth for the Hale Lane Bonfire. A lot of the lads in the group were a few years older than me and I would have been about ten or eleven. Most of the group smoked and as I did not they saw it as weakness.

A lot of the older lads knew about my families religion and if bored would start urging me to smoke to which I would refuse. Then all of a sudden I was grabbed by a few by the older lads and placed in a wooden crate box, which was placed upside down. The crate was a heavy industrial box crate with no lid and they basically had me in a cage with slots in between the timber. As a kid this was a terrifying ordeal and it was about to get worse. They pulled horsehair from a nearby mattress and lit it placing it in the crate with sticks through the gaps. I remember screaming as the box built up with smoke and I was trying to put the fires out. It was hell, and I also remember feeling sharp prods in my side as they poked sticks in with such force I thought I was going to die. All of a sudden I heard my proper mates begging them to let me out. The crate was pulled off me and my mates pulled me up and I walked away with tears in my eyes and a fuel of hate that I would carry for many years.

Over the years in my teens I never forgot one of the older lads who put me through that trauma as it changed me forever. From that day on and for years after I was determined to get my revenge and without a doubt that experience put many demons in my head and made me rebel as a child. I could not understand why I was branded as different because of my families' religion. To me I was no different to anyone else, I never bullied anyone, I never called anyone and I treated my mates and strangers all the same.

This was the world and our society and it was something over time I would learn to adapt to and accept. Out of fear of being bullied and alienated as a young boy I wanted to distance myself from being classed as different, so I did crazy things to grab people's attention which usually involved me getting into trouble.

On the football side of things I had established myself in the school team and it was an honour I used to love. I remember when my dad used to pick me up and ask me how football was and I used to over exaggerate and think he believed me. I would tell him we played Norwich City and Bristol Rovers from some strange reason and he would just smile and roll with it as all fathers do. I cringe now when it think of it!!!

When our kid came up to the juniors we began to have quite a team. Our Louis and his mate Stephen Entwistle were class players and would just waltz around players in the schoolyard games no matter how old they were. When I was in my final year of junior school I was picked for the school team that was entered in the regional school 5 a side tournament. I was really looking forward to it as we had a great team and were fancied favourites. One week before the competition I was expelled from the team for slamming a desk lid on Wayne Hamnets fingers on purpose. He had been mouthing off all day so I just couldn't resist, Mr Johnson the P.E teacher told my mum and although she argued my case I was out and was completely devastated. I had to watch from the sidelines as the team beat Stansfield Road in the final. I was totally distraught and I believe from there I lost my appetite for playing the game.

The following year my brother and his best friend Stephen Entwistle, led a team to win the local five a side cup as well as the Failsworth Junior League Title. So it made it worse that there were two trophies for football on the mantelpiece and not one was mine.

My chosen secondary education was Failsworth Comprehensive School. When I say "chosen" I mean my choice. You see my mum was devastated as she had got me to do the Hulme Grammar entrance exam and everyone was confident (except me) I could get a free place. Don't get me wrong we were far from rich, my mum was a single parent but she would break her back to give Louis and me the best opportunities she could. She even got me my own private tutor! She literally sacrificed all her money and invested in Louis and me. I screamed and shouted with her "I want to go to school with my mates, not some posh nobs from Oldham!! It's my choice" I got my own way and Failsworth Comprehensive it was to be.

Like everyone, you go to your first day at senior school with everyone from your old junior school. Failsworth School was no different, many a grudge were still active due to territorial rivalries that existed. At this time Failsworth was pretty divided with different factions of young lads. South Failsworth was an area where the kids with a few quid lived, mainly what we called top boys at the time, they dressed in sportswear like Fila, Gallini, Ellesse, Sergio Tachinni etc. West Failsworth (Mather Street area) and the Brooks Drive estate was where the rough kids came from, mostly single parents or poor families. This was mainly a punk, mod or skinhead area.

Many of my schoolmates were mods at the time so I was branded as a mod. Although I loved the music I hated the clothes and would just wear jeans and a jumper out of school time. I remember my dad bought me a pair of Kickers from France and a pair of Puma Kenny Dalglish, when I went to the chippy at night with all the young mods the older ones who hung about outside on their scooters would give me grief and go "Look at little Cooper, the top boy, little traitor" I used to buzz off it though, I just wanted to be different and piss them off as they were scruffy glue sniffers in my eyes and I despised their shit clothes compared to the casual scene that was growing by the day.

At Failsworth school the only mods were from Mather Street, so older ex Mather street boys stood out like a sore thumb, Parker jackets, and fish tail coats, while all the top boys wore Adidas cagoules and Farrah pants. (laughed at nowadays)

To my amazement everyone blended really well and I got on like a house on fire with Lads from South Failsworth and Stansfield Road schools. It seemed a funny coincidence how the click became football players but I suppose it's the same in most schools. Over the next few weeks the divide of areas you came from disappeared. Then, as fast as it went a new one appeared and it was City and United.

This only became clear to me on a Friday before a City v United derby day. Everyone brought their scarves to school to show their allegiance to their team, I was flabbergasted. You could feel the tension and the atmosphere. Just before break time I remember seeing a few blues in the toilet smoking saying it was going to kick off City v United. Both were blues who I would get to know very well, Hayden Foy and Anthony Duckworth, Hayden was the only mod I knew from Stansfield Road School and "Ducky" as I called him, was a Blue from Newton Heath. They were both used to taking shit and gave out as good as they got, and were recruiting fellow blues.

That break at school sticks in my mind to this day, Myself, Hayden Foy, Anthony Duckworth, Sharkey, Moggy and loads of other blues surrounded by what seemed like half the school with red scarves. It was all friendly shouting at first with a few songs, but I could see the adrenalin running in the other lad's faces and you just knew one kick would spark it. Next thing it's going right off with people throwing kicks, punches the lot and the annual "Derby Day" mass brawl in a schoolyard was born.

It was one of those mass school fights where you're smiling but throwing "real" punches and 'real' kicks. Someone always goes too far, and in this instance it was Bone. Bone was a passionate blue and his older brother Colin (named after Colin Bell) was a know member of City's hooligan gang in Failsworth. Bone didn't know the meaning of a mess about fight and was unreal considering he weighed about 8 stone at the time. The craziest thing was Bone went to Kaskermoor school and would be truanting it in our school yard at break time and dinner time just looking for a fight.

Then the bell goes and teachers run in to split it up, threats go out

"your getting it later you blue noses"...

"Do one tosser, you don't even go to the game". we would reply

It was just school ground banter but would go on throughout the day, and sometimes start again on Monday unless the game was drawn. From that first fight in school, was born a little click of City fans and the next year we would all travel to the matches together on the 76 bus from Lord Lane bus terminus to Maine Road to watch city's home games together.

With my interest in playing the game all but diminished, I attended City more than ever due to my mum giving me permission to go with Chris Lamb who was one of our neighbours. Chris was a lot older than us and was a top football player as well as being a mad City fan. He would take us to Maine Road and we would sit in the Platt Lane end. Even though Chris lived in the bandit country for "top boys" in Failsworth, he always dressed dead smart and it fascinated me how he dressed the same sort of style as other lads at the match his age. Sometimes I wouldn't watch the match for ages I would just stare at the clothes other City fans our age were wearing. Unbeknown to me, this was the start of the casual scene at City and Platt Lane was full of City lads wearing the top clobber. I would also notice that the ticket touts outside the ticket office who travelled abroad would always have the best gear on and look smart as anything. (Later I would find out it was robbed from abroad)

Over the next few weeks I was begging my mum for a Ski Coat and semi flares, as well as a pair of Adidas Samba and a ski hat. I had to wait till Christmas for the coat, as it was the real deal from Braithwaites Ski shop In Oldham. I remember putting it on in the shop, my first thoughts were about becoming accepted as one of the lads in the Platt Lane. While my mam was paying for the coat I robbed a Ski hat with four tassels on top and I looked and felt like the real football casual. I was that buzzing with the coat I didn't even wear it for school, I just saved it till Saturday. I had also convinced my dad to get me a pair of Samba and semi flares, and on the day of the match I sat and waited for Chris Lamb to knock on the front door kitted out in all my new gear. I was 13 years old but the coat and Adidas Samba made me feel 18. I felt like I was in the uniform of a lad who was about to sign up to war. It was something that made me feel like I was a man and not a young boy anymore.

When we got on the 76 bus it was common occurrence to bump into all my mates from school who were going to the match, and over the next few years I stopped going with Chris who had took me for years and making my own way with Hayden, Ducky, Billy Thug, Moggy and Kevin Sharkey, even our kid and his mates would tag along and sometimes there would be about 20 to 30 of us going to home games. We caused murders on that bus, Graham Davidson, our kids mate was a comedian and used to wind everyone up, including passengers. The more popular we became travelling together, the more fashion conscious everyone became and the casual scene was getting into us.   (That was apart from Hayden Foy who was still kitted out as a mod. I'm sure he thought they were going to make a comeback. Eventually he surpassed us all on the casual look).

At this time in the mid 80's the Platt Lane end was where all City's' lads would gather and I was fascinated by the scene. Our lot were not really into football violence, but we talked about it a lot and it was common occurrence to see a mass fight on the forecourt or the Kippax car park. Piccadilly Gardens was common ground for many battles and we would often sit on the bus upstairs and watch it going off all over the gardens and Oldham Street.. Sometimes Hayden and Ducky would urge everyone to get off the bus, but everyone looked at it as though we were kids and they were men so what's the point???

On the home front our kid was doing really well at football and my mum was on her second marriage. Life was ok, and our step dad Alan treated us well, even though I would bring the police to the door more than once or twice.

At school I was playing for the 'B' team and out of school I was training with Failsworth Tigers. I say train because that's all our kid and me could do, my mum made us go to church on a Sunday and playing football on that day was a major sin. Sunday was the Sabbath day and it was to be respected. Our church was the Latter Day Saints or Mormon as it's known, and the chapel was and still is on Patterdale Road in Ashton. I hated going to church but once I got there I would try to cause murders which made it more enjoyable. We would have Sunday school at first with kids our age that we'd grown up with, then everyone would go into the main chapel and we would have what we call sacrament. I attended church from being aged 5 to 16, and although most of it went in one ear and out the other, I am grateful for having an education of God and the bible, which I believe, put me in good stead for the rest of my life. Like any religion unknown to people who go off gossip, it is falsely know as a 'cult' attended by blokes that give their wages up and who can have seven wives who all come from America. Well, let me tell you nothing could be further from the truth. The church evolves around family values and has a foundation I believe every family on earth would benefit from. Even though I am not a member I still respect it as I do every religion that doesn't enforce itself upon people and kill and start wars in the name of God. Anyway, that was our church and football was out for Sundays, but to compensate my mum would take us to a midweek meeting for the church youth, where we played indoor football with other church kids.

At this time I started getting the taste for playing again, and I was on the verge of the "A" team at school. I had scored a 30-yard goal against Grange school for the "B" team and Mr Tyrell told me I was to prepare myself for the call-up. I was buzzing; the "A" team had some class players such as Dave Donnigan, Steve Mercer, Paul Jolley, Jason Tynan, Todd Littlewood and Andy Derbyshire. These were all my mates and class players but I was yet to convince them I was "A" team material. The game I made my debut in was against local rivals Kaskenmoor High. This was a bit of a grudge match as they were literally a mile up the road and we would meet them now and again at dinner time and have running battles with them. I was named substitute and in the dressing room I got a bit of banter for coming from the B team. I was determined to prove them wrong, about 30 minutes into the game Jason Tynan got injured and I was called into midfield to replace him. I was nervous as hell and could feel the uncertainty of the other players as I walked onto the pitch. Midfield wasn't my position, I was a centre half but I'd gone past caring. I was like a bull in a china shop. I just went in tackle after tackle, getting the ball and giving it the more skilful players who could do something with it. I played like your modern day Vinny Jones, and was booked in the second half and told by the manager (the late) Mr Potter to calm it down. The game finished 1-1 but I knew I had proved a point, and was congratulated by the manager. A few of the players came over like Andy Derbyshire, Paul Jolley and Steve Mercer and gave me the old well done, pat on the back, good game shout. Sadly, it was the last game of the season and it was my last game for the school "A" team. (Apart from me being crap)

I was to suffer a bad tear in my cruciate ligament ice-skating while on a church youth camp at Linnet Clough Scout Camp 3 weeks later. I was on crutches for a month and limping for about 4 months and regularly had to go to hospital for physio to build the muscle up again. For me it never felt the same, and I never felt the same player tackling or being tackled as it always felt weak. With that I stopped attending Failsworth Tigers and stopped playing even for the school B team which I loved.

My playing days were over (how professional ha ha) and I slowly drifted away from my mates who played the game, I was to take another path in my football life and meet new friends and experience a lot of travelling. My focus was now on doing everything possible to be a football casual....or in other words a Young Guvnor! I did try break dancing as I loved the fashion attached to it but it was like too much hard work. I loved listening to the music and listened to a lot of stuff like public enemy, LL Cool Jay, Eric B and Rakeem, but having a "dance off" on a piece of lino when you had an argument was something I could never understand.

After being bullied from a young age I started to fight back and I quickly realised I was more than capable of fighting and defending myself. In fact it got to a point where I truly believe fighting solved everything.

In the 1980's, the football casual scene was exploding and it pulled me in like most other lads of my age due to the feeling of being part of something. The fashion sense was like nothing I had ever seen, and it was a big factor in me becoming involved in the casual explosion.

CHAPTER TWO

" ONE OF THE LADS"

I must put in this chapter something that I feel is relevant to the way Europeans looked at us as a nation in the football hooligan days of the 80's and 90's. An old mate of mine, Fitzy from Moston in Manchester, told me this story about when he was on holiday once....

One night in the hotel we were staying in, they were holding an "international quiz" and wanted three people from three different countries to compete against each other. I'm a proud Englishman so straight away I went to the front. After a quiet chat with me and the two other volunteers, the compare introduced us to the audience. "Ladies and Gentleman, our first contestant is Jan from Holland.... the great country that gave us windmills, tulips and clogs. Our second contestant is Francois from France, the great country that gave us the Eiffel Tower, The Mona Lisa, Romance and Champagne. Our third contestant is Fitzy from England - AND HE WILL KICK YOUR HEAD INNNNNN"

With me losing interest in playing the game, I rapidly increased watching the game. I was about 14 years of age when I gave up playing football, and my mum was more than happy for me to go to the match as long as I went as a group with my mates, half the reason was City played in Moss Side and it was still known as a rough area of Manchester.

Our Louis usually still played football on a Saturday with Failsworth Tigers, and he was one less thing to worry about on a match day. I was now regularly attending with Hayden Foy, Anthony Duckworth and Paul Coleman (aka Billy Thug) every home game, with probably another fourteen or fifteen Failsworth lads.

Over the years we would travel to every home match and also local away matches such as Everton, Liverpool, Oldham, Notts County and of course Man United. We would always be standing and have the best times of our lives rammed in pens and swaying with the crowds giving abuse to opposing fans and the local plod.

I remember being able to pay in at Old Trafford on Derby Day's, such as when Ian Brightwell scored a screamer against Jim Leighton, 8000 City fans were rammed in the paddock behind the net and it was the best goal celebration ever. We always had a knack of coming from behind at Old Trafford, and if you ask any blue from back in those days it was like a win for us, and a loss for them.

When City scored you just got carried from where you were stood and sometimes ended up 5 or 6 metres away in all the euphoria. It was mental; it was a true football high I don't sadly feel anymore! Fans would congregate in the ground up to 2 hours before the kick off, to bellow out songs to each other's end. Derby days in the late 80's and early 90's were the best atmosphere I have ever experienced. The noise was phenomenal and it did make your hairs stand up on the back of your neck. Both sets of fans would sing "Hark now hear" full belt at each other with the whole ends singing. You were on pins for ninety inutes watching the match, and would come out of the ground with your voice gone. People say football then was in the dark ages, but now I look back it was in its prime for atmosphere! The prices to get in, the atmosphere, the working class feel, and the amount of young kids there, cheap away travel. I just don't see any of that in today's modern game?

In 1985 City played United at Maine Road in the first BBC Live Derby weekend game. It was played in front of a crowd of only 33,000, which was unheard of for a derby game. Peter Swales in his wisdom had made the game all ticket and you could only get a ticket if you had six home vouchers. At the time none of our Failsworth lot took the vouchers seriously and it stopped a lot of us getting a ticket. Somehow I managed to get a ticket from somewhere and attend the game on my own. Tony Grealish was making his debut for City and was up against the formidable Bryan Robson who was making a name for himself at United. I think he notched a goal to open the scoring, but good old Mick McCarthy scored with a bullet header from the edge of the penalty area to equalise. At the end of the game I remember seeing it kick off unlike anything I'd ever seen outside the City Social Club. Two groups of about 200 lads just fighting like hell.

The City lads stood out, as I knew a few faces I had come to recognise over the years and a lot were local black and mixed raced lads. (I was later to learn that this was the "Maineline" firm of Manchester City and Uniteds Red Army) I was infatuated with the roar and the uncertainty and the mass confusion it caused, and how smart all the lads looked. I knew then that's what I wanted to do, who I wanted to be with on match days and how I wanted to dress.

I remember in school on the Monday talking to Ducky and Hayden about what I had experienced and seen. We were all in agreement we would start looking for the Maineline firm and tag along and see what we could see.

Over the next two or three years we did exactly that and would tag along at the back of a firm of say 150 lads. A lot would tell us to piss off and go back to school, but we would stand our ground and just carry on following. Paul Coleman's older brother Colin was in the older City firm and we used to always look for him and his other friends who were Lee Boots, Scott, Aki and Lee Pickup in town before a game so they would lead us to the firm. It really used to annoy them and I remember a few times Colin would be kicking Paul up the arse and telling him to "Do one and go home"

It wasn't until 1989 that I was involved in my first actual fight at a football match, yes, we had bounced around behind the older lads for years but we never got stuck in as we just weren't confident. I had just started at college doing plumbing that year and the big game was talked about for weeks in advance. City played Chelsea at Maine Road in a Division Two title decider, and United were playing Nottingham Forest in the FA Cup at Old Trafford on the same day. For some weird reason the police allowed it to go on, and gave it their blessing that both matches could be played on the same day. Every football lad in Manchester was well aware of what was going to happen and it would be an eventful day.

The day of the Chelsea game I remember knocking on for Paul Coleman at 10am in the morning, five hours before the match. His dad answered the door with a smile and let me in shouting up the stairs for Paul to get up as he went in the kitchen to do us a brew. The Coleman's old man was a lovely fellow, he originally lived on Maine Road when he was a kid and was City daft. I always remember him being dressed dead smart, taking his time grooming his hair in the mirror with a cig in his mouth. He would wear a shirt and tie with a pair of top notch gold cuff links just to go shopping and always looked like an old time mafia godfather.

While I would wait for Paul to get ready, Colin would always try and belittle him like all brothers do in front of his mates. He would clip him and tell him not to wear his clothes and stay away from him and his mates at the match. That house was where I heard for the first time the term 'Guvnor' for a City boy. Colin told us both about the "Young Guvnors" and we should get in with them and leave him and the older lot alone. I'd seen the Young Guvnors sprayed on walls in town and written on buses in marker pen but never related it to City. As we left the house we discussed the Young Guvnors and later with Ducky and Hayden Foy, I was determined to be involved in the Young Guvnors, and my first introduction with them came quicker than I expected.

After meeting Hayden and Ducky we got the 82 bus to town down Oldham Road. We would usually do this if we thought it was a tasty fixture and leave the rest of the Failsworth Blues who were basically straight goers to get the 76 direct to Maine Road. The 82 stopped at the lights outside the Crown and Kettle at the junction of Great Ancoats Street, and we all quickly noticed a large firm of United outside the Top Yates Wine Lodge (now the Frog and Bucket Comedy Club) spilling into the street drinking. A few were staring up at the bus and Ducky did not hesitate to give them the finger as we drove past them. As the bus drove up Oldham Street towards Piccadilly Gardens we noticed another large mob, which we knew, must have been City. They were just stood underneath the statue of Queen Victoria as though they were waiting for the shout. I remember Ducky running off the bus shouting to them all "United are up here at Yates, come on" Everyone just looked at us like a bunch of idiots. It was obvious that everyone knew and there was something planned.   I was a bit embarrassed and noticed a few faces in the firm who went to my college doing Plumbing and Bricklaying courses. Johnny Gunnings, Slicker, Colin Jones, Cozzi, Marco Rossi, Rodney Rhoden were all members of the Mills Hill Villains from Chadderton. They were all Mancs but like Failsworth, hated by everyone from Oldham as they were constantly battling with lads like Lee Spence, Jay Martin and Scott Morley from Oldhams F.Y.C. at a club called Butterflys in Oldham.

We just blended in and I introduced the Failsworth lads to them all and asked what was going on. Before I got an explanation we were moving, but were told to split into two groups. The Young Guvnors were to be the bait with the Older Guvnors in back Piccadilly coming from the side., within 20 seconds United were in front of us and it went off for about 30 or 40 seconds before a convoy of police vans steamed into both sets of fans. Everyone got split up, and the police just waded into everyone hitting us all, red or blue with their small truncheons. More and more police came into the gardens just wading into us but there were still pockets of reds and blues kicking off with each other all over the place.

After that game and getting to know the Mills Hill Villains, I started going to the game more with my mate from college Johnny Gunnings. He was a funny character and was City daft and was more connected with people inside the Guvnors than anyone of my lot from Failsworth.

Over the next few years Johnny and the M.H.V. would introduce me to the other Young Guvnors like Jamie Roberts, Yozzer, Smythes, Peter Wright, Dennis Bradley and a lot of the Rusholme and Moss Side boys. I remember getting on to their fashion sense and they all had these £200 Berghaus or Sprayway Coats. They looked quality, and as well as being all weather, which was ideal for the match they were more than fashionable and were more than passable to get you in clubland. I bought my first one, which was a dark green three quarter Sprayway from the Newton Heath shoplifters for £45 and I was buzzing. The Crown in Newton Heath was a haven for shoplifters, as they would go all over the country and rob the best designer gear. Then they would return to the pub and sell it for a third of the price. That pub basically clothed every lad in Failsworth and Newton Heath for the next decade and sometimes it was a live auction with all the local workers going in at 5pm bidding on clothes.

As I mixed more with the Young Guvnors we went clubbing together and most times we would go to the legendary Cyprus Tavern or the old Brannigans in St Annes Square. They were our two main nightspots for a while, but things were changing. The Madchester rave scene was upon us and we started to go to the Thunderdome, Hacienda, Konspiracy, The House, Precinct 13, Legends and a little club in China Town called Shenza's. This was more of a bar than a club but it played music and that's all that mattered. It was in there that I was to meet one of my best mates at the match, Burnsy. I remember walking in and him staring at me, but then he realised who I was with. He told me he thought I was...

"Man Yoo innit"...

to which I just frowned at him and carried on mimicking his funky chicken dance. With Burnsy being from Wythenshawe I started being introduced to more lads from the south side of Manchester such as Brogan, Colin Little, Kieron M and Ady M. Sometimes we would go clubbing and there would be up to sixty or seventy of us in a club and we literally went all over the northwest, from Sequins in Blackpool to Shelly's in Stoke to Maximes in Wigan... all top nights but 95% of the time there was always fighting.

If it weren't with us it would be Cheetham Hill, Moss Side or Salford fighting each other. When it was one of those three firms we learnt not to get involved as it was usually over money or drugs and nothing at all to do with football. When those three firms (I mean the real firm and not just residents of the areas) walked in a club usually one of us knew one or two of their faces and we just had a chat and steered clear or gave them the space they wanted. People say ecstasy cooled down the hooligan scene but I say that's a load of rubbish, we all still went all over the country fighting anyone, and the opposing firms were exactly the same.

People think the club scenes mad now, but then it was common occurrence for doorman to get shot or minced every week. It was big money having doors in those days, because if you had the doors you had the run of drugs being sold in the club.   It was during this time that Operation Omega happened and City's older firm were raided, Jamie Roberts, Ady Gunnings and Rodney Rhoden were nicked out of the Young Firm and Mickey and Chris Francis and twelve others out of the older lot, all received stiff sentences in jail. After that over the next few years there was no real organisation with City's firm so we just used to jump on the Parkside coach to away matches.

The Parkside pub was situated right outside City's ground and their coach trips were to give me some of the funniest experiences of my life. There was one game we went to against Crystal Palace at Selhurst Park, it was the quarter finals of the league cup. On arriving in Croyden fifty of us walked in an off licence and Dennis Bradley asked for 20 B+H, as soon as the shop assistant turned round everyone just filled their pockets. All you could hear was the clinking of bottles. The poor young girl who was serving couldn't do a thing and as Dennis got his cigs we all left the shop to go to the pub. The first pub we found was an Irish pub on the corner of the street, and as we entered I noticed a big throne at one end of the pub. I sat on it and everyone decided to put their robbed spirits and beer underneath as I sat on it posing like a king absolutely bladdered after drinking for a solid four hours on the coach.

About fifteen minutes later the police turned up and an inspector came in the boozer with about ten old bill. They looked about and the inspector approached me and asked me if I was having a good time and seemed quite polite giving City fans compliments. As I was drunk I thought nothing of it, but then he asked me, "Where's your mate with the cap?" to which I replied, "Who Burnsy he's over there playing pool".

As soon as I said that the inspector pulled a video cassette out and looked at me and said "Well done lad, you've been framed robbing the off licence, you're under arrest!"

I was ill and Burnsy was fuming calling me a thick get for grassing him up. All the way to the police station he was hounding me as I was laughing and apologising to him, I was totally drunk out of my head as I staggered to the van in handcuffs. After two hours at the station they cautioned us and let us out at half time on the condition we went back to the off licence and paid the bill for what had been nicked. We both agreed as we didn't want to miss the coach home and just nodded to everything they were telling us to do. When we got back to the ground Burnsy was walking towards the off licence, when I said "What you doing?" ...he was ready for paying the off-licence back until I convinced him that the coppers were taking the mickey out of him! City got hammered 4-1 and that was always the case when we had a big match, the team let the fans down.

On the way home we did the same thing in the service station, but this time it was just cooked sausages and everything out of the shop. The girl who was serving food went in the kitchen and everyone lent over the glass counter which just smashed to pieces due to the weight of five lads on it. We all made a run for the coach laughing our heads off but then five miles down the motorway the coach got stopped off the police and we were all ill.

As the coach stopped for some strange reason the police cars radio interfered with the coach radio and we heard the station's instructions to the driver "Yes, we're looking for two males aged 20 to 30 both of mixed race about 5"11 and 6"0" Everyone on the coach pissed themselves as Franny Charles and Smythes made a dash for the toilets and hid. Nigel Forshaw let the traffic copper on and he walked up and down with everyone holding back laughing. It was like that scene in the Life of Brian where Caesar says "Biggus Dickus" to the guards. The copper looked a right slime ball and was a double of the prison guard Mr McKye out of Porridge, he knew something was wrong as none of us could look at him. Reluctantly he got off the coach and let us go and as we pulled off the police interference on the coach radio let us hear him confirm to the station that there was no bodies of that description on the coach, the full coach was in fits of laughter. I could seriously write a full chapter on the events and funny experiences I encountered with the Parkside Coach. It was full of the funniest and best characters at the match I ever met. You were guaranteed a laugh and a top day out. They've now re-named it "The Shameless Coach" after the T.V programme. If as a blue you ever get the chance to go to an away match jump on it and have a ball!

Over the next few years on the pitch City would struggle and go through over ten managers and three divisions. The thing was, it never deterred any blues from going because if you were a City fan you went for the day, the atmosphere, the characters and now and then you might see some half decent football.

Maine Road was a major part of being a blue, it was our spiritual home and I believe it still is. In the 80's I used to love the old wooden Platt Lane, it could hold 8000 and was divided from the Kippax by a concrete corner. I always remember the Piccadilly 261 sign over its entrance and watching as away fans got soaked in the rain. The atmosphere in the Platt Lane end was quality and it was rammed with lads.

I remember Leeds and Everton tried storming it through the bottom gate but were both unsuccessful, and ended up with some bad casualties.

The old Kippax was just like a big bus shelter that held 32,000 people, it was so basic now I look back its hard to believe. Many great memories in there, like when we beat Charlton 5-1 and got promoted. The official attendance that day was something like 48,000, but if you ask anyone who was in the Kippax that day they will tell you that's was a load of crap. You could not move in there and every other stand was rammed. I still believe to this day that there was nearly 60,000 in that ground as it was bursting at the seams. Even the away end was full of City fans as the Platt Lane end was over spilling. That's one of the reasons I really believe people don't understand the potential of City and its support base. I still to this day am adamant if you gave City a 60,000 capacity stadium and put the prices right down to accommodate everyone you would fill it!

If I could take my two kids and me to the match for £20 for all of us I would do it every week and I also believe thousands of others would. I had a discussion with a big red once and he was saying that when we moved to Eastland's we would never fill it, as we just had 30,000 and that was our lot. I bet him £100 we would average 47,000 a week and I won (Stand forward Buckethead)

Another great game was the 5-1 against United in the late 1980's, I remember the atmosphere was electric and I was five yards away (due to segregation) from all the Failsworth Reds in the away end in the Kippax. Local reds who I knew, Gav Pinder, Wolfy, Grimmy were all throwing the banter from the away end of the Kippax five foot away from me and I was not confident of us winning as United were fielding a team of £22 million pound.

I watched and jumped for joy as one goal went in after the other... and let me tell you it's the best feeling watching your mates faces as your team score goal after goal against their big time Charlie's. I was close to tears of joy and it was an unreal feeling walking out of the ground that day as the media had given us no chance.

Over the years as the Kippax and Platt Lane were flattened and replaced with modern stands, all the singers and lads moved into the North stand and the Maine Stand. I would go in the Maine Stand as the Parkside lads had taught me the art of "Jibbing in" and "Doubling up. To jib in you would just hurdle over the turnstiles and leg it up the concrete stairs 95% of the time you got in, but now and again you would get your foot stuck in the turnstile depending on how pissed you were.

As you got older you doubled up, and to do this you would prowl about outside and wait for a city fan in the queue who was young or quite thin and go in behind them. As soon as you heard the turnstile click you would squeeze up and go in as one. Most of the Parkside all did this, home and away for over 15 years, they were the masters at it. Some amateurs would pick fat City fans to double up with and would get stuck and it used to be funny as hell watching the turnstiles from the bar.

There were occasions where some other amateurs picked women and you would often hear screams from the turnstiles as the woman would be thinking she was getting manhandled as a young lad was pushing her arse up trying to double up. Once we were in we would watch pure young lads bolting over and getting legged by stewards up the stairs. Then, because the steward had gone in pursuit another 15 or so would bolt over and the turnstile collector would just give up. That was part of the day and I would love to go back in time with CCTV and show the best jibbers and the worst jibbers, it would get thousands of hits on Youtube.

Once we got in the Maine Stand all the lads would sit in the top left hand corner behind the police surveillance box. It was customary to smell every brand of weed being smoked on the market, from black, spuds, pollen, sess and of course the Rusholme bread of life "BUD".

I remember once, at a midweek game it was a really low attendance and there were only about ten of us in the corner in the Maine Stand. A lad was sat next to us who I didn't know but a few of the others knew him so I just got talking to him. He was constantly up and down and seemed a really passionate City fan. At half time he had a few drags of the Rusholme "BUD" he had been passed off Kinnak and he didn't say a word in the second half he was ruined! I remember a blue called Scully saying to me did I know who it was to which I replied no, he told me it was his mates out of a new band called Oasis, he introduced us but I wasn't much into music so it went over my head, plus I was stoned. I later realised after seeing them on T.V sometime later it was Liam Gallagher, and I just had a giggle to myself. He seemed a decent lad and I found out later on in life Liam's brother Noel used to go all over with City and was well respected with a lot of the Guvnors from Levenshulme, Gorton, Burnage and Rusholme.

When we went for a beer at the match, as well as the Parkside pub we would go in the Sherwood, Lord Lyon, Clarence and The Albert. Usually these were the boozers for meets for everyone if we were expecting any opposing teams lads making a visit. When we were at Maine Road this happened basically every week and it must have been a horrible ground for away fans to visit. It was just a maze of back alleys, rat runs and side streets, which was ideal for us. I could go on and on about the battles but books and people have already done that so it doesn't need writing again.

Sometimes I would just think we were the defence regiment of Manchester City football fans, and if anyone ever tried taking liberties with them or us we would meet them head on and return the favour.

There was one instance when we played West Brom away and few of our lads got ambushed in a car park by over forty of their lads. Brad Doyle, Paul from Monton and eight of the young firm were surrounded and had a right fight. They basically had to stand their ground for over twenty minutes with West Broms lads taking liberties.

The next season we travelled with about 150 away to their ground and made sure we paid them back, by staying till 8 o'clock at night. There was that much fun and games, when the police escorted City to the tram station their lads applauded our lot from on the bridge!

While attending the match over the years I got nicked a few times with fines and banned once or twice. As you go more you get wiser to the way the police move, think and their tactics. They'll come over to you, say your name, and give you a smile trying to be your mate. They do it with every known lad in the country but wouldn't give you the time of day if they had the first chance to nick you. There's tales of them offering lads season tickets to inform them of movements of large numbers and plans for away trips. Also lots of other little tactics like offering deals before court cases and stitching other lads up.

I look back at my involvement over the years and people say to me football lads are all scumbags and what's the big attraction. I have sat down and asked myself the question a few times but always had an answer, when I was a young kid I always wanted to join the army, I think it was mainly because I was infatuated with a comic hero in a magazine for kids called "Warlord". Warlord was a comic full of stories about soldiers fighting in the armed forces. The main character I would read about was a guy who was English but served in the US Royal Marines. His name was "Union" Jack Jackson and he would always wear a union jack on his helmet.

He was always pulling the yanks out of the shit and pounding the Japanese or the Germans. He was the soldier every young kid at junior school wanted to be and I bet loads of people joined up through his and the comics influence on young kids.

Ask yourself this, why do people want to join the army? What attracts young people to join our armed forces? Think about it! I came up with these answers

To fire a gun

To feel part of something important

To do your service and represent your country (or club in our case)

To travel

To look smart in your uniform

For the adventure

For the discipline and respect

Now if you can add any then go ahead, if you replace "Country" with "Manchester" apart from maybe the last one that's exactly what attracted me to be a football lad, swap the gun for a punch and that's the same list as I had in my head at sixteen years of age and I am being totally honest. I gave up on the army when I was fifteen as my parents wouldn't sign my form to gain access and I had changed my mind when I was sixteen as I was totally football mad, watching and following all over the country. I was basically in a part time army where I would meet other lads who would become great friends and loved as brothers. See places I would otherwise never have seen and meet people and had experiences that I would have only dreamed of.

Today the scene is totally different with heavy sentences and police harassment and CCTV killing the football lad's unity of yesteryear. In my eyes now it is probably a great thing for football as you see more fans at the match and definitely more families...

but in the same breath less deprived kids being able to afford to attend. One thing we have all noticed though is that more street gangs are appearing all over the country which are using territories and boundaries to make their stamp. Instead of using their fists like we did they are using knives and guns and literally killing each other every day of the week. As I write this book we are in July 2008 and up to now, nineteen people have been killed in this country through being stabbed, 90% of them are under the age of eighteen! I have read countless articles in the press and watched on lots of television documentaries, testimonies of gang members describing it's all about turf and respect. "If some one comes on your side of the street you make sure they never want to come back" Mainly this is happening in London and its not that bad in Manchester as we speak but I expect to see it duplicated up here soon enough as the Government seems to be doing nothing.

I believe it's because they haven't got a clue what to do and how to do it. I believe the solution is sport and I have always believed that from day one. Sport is the answer to every problem because it is open to everyone, it took me twenty years to realise how much of a great tool sport and especially football can be.

When we went to football we didn't take knives or any tools and we never kicked anyone on the floor. There was one particular game against Bradford away where we had a huge battle in their town centre. The previous week they had been rowing with United in the cup and had gained a fair bit of respect. During the fighting some of their lads fell on their arses and a few of us pulled them up and patted them down and said, "don't worry mate we don't do lads on the deck". Both lads seemed a little shocked and went their merry way in disbelief. A few young lads on the train said they wouldn't have done that if it was us on the floor, but we argued that City didn't do shithouse tricks and that was that.

The next season we played them in a night match, which I didn't attend due to work. Anyway I get a phone call from two mates from Miles Platting called Dave Hazelwood and Matt Grandon who went to the match. They told me this little story...

So we come off the station and go in the first pub we see for a beer as its two hours before kick off. There are only 8 of us and we're all sat having a quiet one for about an hour. Then all of a sudden 40 Bradford walk in and order themselves some beers. Everything goes quiet and we're thinking it's going right off here, we better get ready as we knew who they were and they knew who we were. All of a sudden one walks over with a bit of a smile "You Man City lads?" We answered, "yes" just thinking here we go!! He replies.... " sweet lads, we had a top row with your lot last season and a couple of our lads were on the floor but your lot were sweet and made sure they didn't get a kicking on the deck or got massacred so you've got no worries in here today". When Dave told me this on the phone I couldn't believe it! I nearly choked on my tea... Dave, Matt and the other lads were not really hooligans but could have a "read and write". It just hit me in the face how different it all could have been......... "WHAT GOES AROUND, COMES AROUND"

Dave said they had a good drink with them, and 3 weeks later two of them even turned up at court when we had a few lads who were up on charges that were eventually all cleared.

Sometimes though it does not always work like that, and some lads from all over the country have been ruined for life and some have even lost their lives. Every lad in the country who has ever been involved with his own particular firm will confirm to you that it can be like running a gauntlet sometimes and some really nasty things can happen. So if you're a young lad thinking this was and is a game, and its toy fighting, then be warned...It was a war every weekend home and away and people suffered including the lads kids, wives and parents. Do you think the police would use eighty officers to escort firms of 100 to 150 lads if they thought it was a game?

Another thing I learnt about football lads fast was that if a firm had one hundred lads then no matter who they were only the first twenty would actually fight. The rest would just bounce, and I saw that with every football firm we ever came across in the country.

As you get older you become more and more involved as part of that twenty which taught you that a lot of times numbers meant nothing. It was more about the heart and courage of your first twenty lads that made the difference. Sometimes when I was young I would often wonder why the older lads would just walk off with thirty lads and leave a firm of two hundred. Even if we were expecting a big away turnout the older ones would always try and break off and leave us as the police decoy. Nine times out of ten it would work and later on in the day we'd find out that had been exactly what had happened.

As we became older it was becoming more and more apparent to us all that the Guvnors had no organisation at all. We had pockets of little firms in different pubs all around the ground and the only time we got together was at the Sherwood after the match when the visiting team was scouted with a big firm. Every lad knew that we had the potential to be a huge firm but no one was prepared to do any sort of leadership, and who could blame them. The last lads who tried to do that were jailed in Operation Omega and were still serving banning orders.

I decided something needed to be done so I arranged a do for all City's lads at a pub on Princess Street in the City Centre called "The Overdraught". It was directly facing the Cyprus Tavern that had been a city centre club frequented by many City lads over the years. I arranged for two strippers and hired a DJ as well as a comedian.

The DJ was the drummer out of the band Inspiral Carpets called Gilly. He was a good lad and a friend of a mate called Tony Rowan who gave me a lift organising it. The comedian was a late replacement and his name was "Bobby Bender" I got 300 tickets printed and I think I sold the tickets for £3 or something. They went like wildfire and I was sold out a week before the event, which was after our Saturday fixture against Leeds United at home.

I got another 200 tickets printed and sold them on the day. Right after the game I got a taxi straight to The Overdraught and started setting everything up and had my friend Tony Rowan doing the door. Within 10 minutes of us arriving there were five police TAG unit vans outside the venue. The weird thing was though they never came in the place, they just watched as more and more City lads entered the building. As well as taking tickets I told Tony to take cash as well and not turn anyone away as I wanted everyone to see the numbers we could achieve.

An hour before the strippers were due on, the place was absolutely heaving. The manager of the place was looking at me with his finger pointing at his head giving me the mental sign. Gilly the DJ was belting out tunes like "The Clash, The Stone Roses, The Jam, The Specials, The Sex Pistols, Big Audio Dynamite, Oasis" the place was going mental with a mixture of City songs. There was easily over six hundred lads in the place with about twenty to thirty stood outside smoking Moss Side's finest. I had to hire my mate Charlie Sow from Moss Side for security for the strippers and he did himself proud. Charlie was an old school "Cool Cat" and is a huge man who is a good friend. He had respect and was someone you did not want a right hook off as it was likely to take your head clean off. He still does the door today at Mickey Francis's pub near city's ground "The Guvnor" say hello to him he's a gent.

With the place rammed and the crowd getting uneasy I had to grab the microphone and be the MC, was nervous as hell. Some of these lads were huge men and out of the 600 I only knew about 150. The rest I didn't have a clue about, but I just thought fuck it, it's now or never.

"Right everyone, I've organised this do to get us all together to have a few beers, see some tits and have a laugh" Everyone cheered really loud, the place was absolutely mental, beer was spilt everywhere with the smell of weed and cocaine burning in the air. "I'd like to introduce the comedian Boooooobbbbbeeeeee Beeeeennnnddeeeeer" Again everyone went mad with a huge cheer. Bobby Bender came out and his appearance was that of an 80's snooker player with a leather waistcoat and a grey buffoon haircut. He looked terrified, and I really believe the audience sensed it, as he grabbed the microphone off me..

"Thank you Thank You...Have you heard the one about the new lesbian sneakers called Alldykes? Sales dropped dramatically when customers found the tongues weren't long enough"

You could hear a pin drop, I just looked at all the City lads and it was like they were waiting for the punch line. All I could hear was glasses clinking and a few orders being given at the bar. I thought to myself say another crap joke and the next minute's silence will be for you mate!

"Two children were playing on the beach with their dog when a freak wave carried the poor animal out to sea. Luckily, a passing German backpacker saw the plight of the dog so he dived in and dragged it from the water, laid it on the sand and gave it mouth-to-mouth resuscitation.

"Are you a vet?" asked the children.

"vet?" replied the German... "I'm soaking"

The place went up, everyone was in hysterics and I was more than relieved to say the least. I thought sweet I'll go and check how Charlie is with the strippers. The girls were getting ready in the kitchen of all places and funnily enough smoking Moss Sides finest like many of the audience. I gave them and Charlie instructions and after 10 minutes I went back out to check how Bobby was doing.

I looked out the door in absolute shock to see Brad Doyle from Salford with the comedians microphone in his hand telling jokes. He had taken the microphone off the comedian and poor old Bobby was just stood their deflated. Doyley is a huge frame of a man and hard as nails, no one was going to take the microphone off him and to be fair he was doing quite well. The place was chaos for an hour but everyone just started singing City songs and everyone was in good spirits. Then I go to check Tony Rowans ok at the entrance door,

"You ok Rowan?" I asked,

"Sound mate but your not" he replied,

"Why what's wrong mate"

I looked at him and thought I was going to get the end of one of his jokes, "Gilly the DJ has done one mate, I think he either had another appointment or he thought it was a bit radio rental (mental) but the best is, he had to take his jack leads and now we've got no turntables connected to the amp" I just froze.......... What the hell was I going to do, no music for the strippers? I had 500 of Citys hardcore lads waiting for the strippers and things would get ugly if they did not perform. My head was in pieces, I just squeezed myself through all the lads making my way to the strippers in the kitchen as lads patted me on the back, the full room was in a chorus of "We are City from Maine Road" at full volume.

"Belting do this Cooper", "Well done lad, when are the strippers out?"

My head was gone, I was thinking no music - no strippers! I'm going to get lynched here. I got in the kitchen and informed the strippers,

"You are joking aren't ya?"

Charlie and the strippers just started laughing at me as he leant on the cooker smoking a bit of their spliff with moss side's finest taking full effect on them.

"Give me 10 minutes girls and I swear I will sort it out"

I rushed through the crowd to the DJ booth to check if there was something I could do. Pure people were pecking at my head,

"Why are we waiting...oh whyyyy...."

The lads were getting really pissed off and I could sense it. I was that desperate I even told Brad Doyle and Salford John to tell more jokes they just looked at me and laughed. Then I felt a tap on the shoulder, Mr Williams the manager held up a small tape recorder,

"What am I supposed to do with that, are you having a laugh or what?"

The noise was deafening and I thought I had misheard him; I looked at him like he was as thick as two short planks!

The look was returned…..

"Use your head and turn it on, then play it through the microphone and it will go through the PA system."

He just smiled sarcastically but I knew where he was coming from, what did I have to loose apart from my full head. I grabbed the tape recorder off him, pressed eject and slipped in one of the strippers tapes they had given me, I grabbed the microphone and pointed it at the speaker of this little £25 portable stereo and pressed play…….

"Should I stay or should I go now………"

The place went mental as The Clash boomed out of the PA system, the microphone volume was on full and I just looked at Williams the manager and give him the thumbs up. Happy Days I thought.

The strippers did their dance and I had to stand for 15 minutes holding a microphone at this piece of crap but it worked and the night went quality.

Bobby Bender never came back on, he said to me in the kitchen…

"Listen lad, I've played all over the country in some of the worst places ever, but I can't do a second stint out their mate, I could die!"

He still wanted his money though! The strippers were ok , they had Big Charlie looking after them but Bobby's only protection was the microphone and Doyley had that so we felt sorry for him and sorted him out. (He still waited in the kitchen till the place emptied).

At the end of the stripper show the manager came over to me with a concerned look..

"Listen how the hell am I going to get 500 lunatics out of here, I've got to clean up for the club night which starts in half an hour?"

I looked at him and smiled

"Watch this"...... I replied and gave him a reassuring smile.

"Listen lads, I hope you've all had a great night, but the manager has got another function on tonight so we have to clear the room, but don't worry because we've just heard United are back from Bradford now so we will go for a drink with them on Deansgate"

Within 60 seconds the place was empty, the lot of us only got to Albert Square and the police were waiting heavy handed in their robo cop uniforms and just waded into us for no reason whatsoever, batons, horses, the lot and it got really messy. Still to this day it baffles me as we only went for a drink in our city yet we weren't arrested, just charged at for no reason. Without doubt there must have been undercover police in the bar watching the strippers, I was later told that the strippers did not go the full monty as you had to have a licence for them to go all the way and the manager had made sure that didn't happen.

Due to the success of that event over the years I organised a good few more with proceeds going to good causes. One was for "The Set Up Six" who were a bunch of City lads who received jail terms of up to 3 years for a fight with some Stockport lads in the city centre. It always baffled me how society could give such sentences when during the same year a convicted paedophile in Sussex received an 18 month suspended sentence for having over 7000 images of children on his pc? No one was injured in the fight and a few lads did not even get round to throwing a punch. Yet there lives were destroyed with some of them losing their jobs, their partners, and in some cases their homes. You can say they knew what they were doing and its breaking the law, but if that's the case then the paedophile with the images should be getting 9 years jail in my eyes.

We also organised "The Set Up Six Boxing Brawl" at Mike Francis's Champagne Charlies Bar. We hired a boxing ring and made a card up of fights between lads I knew from going to the match over the years. The set up was top notch and my mate Dave Hazlewood and Gary at "Ringmasters" did us a reduced rate for the ring and sorted us a mint PA system out.

All the young firm at City were well up for it and word went round like wildfire. Tickets sold like hot cakes and I went to my old boxing gym in Clayton called Northside, to purchase a few sets of sparring gloves and head guards from Joe Pennington. Joe's another feller who I look up to and is a local legend, the guy dedicates his life to moulding kids off the street to become disciplined fighters that show respect out of the ring, but no respect in the ring.

We also arranged for the boxer "Michael Gomez" to attend and got another top comedian. The place was hammered on the day and everything went better than expected. I did the role of MC as well as having a few rounds with my mate "Fitzy" who's an absolute star and a belting lad.

Most of the fights were absolute street brawls especially the fight between two of the young lads called Reidy and Danials, but with the sparring gloves and head guards no one was going to do any major damage only to their lungs. The funniest fight was one between two of the biggest lads "Special K" and a lad from Sale called Brains. Both were top lads and good friends, but "K" was representing the Northside blues and "Brains" representing the Southside blues. Brains had even had a belt made for the event and strapped a tinned "Fray Bentos" pie to it. Every fighter came out to music that I was in control of, usually things like "I'm gonna knock you out by LL Cool J", "White Riot by The Clash" and Eye of the Tiger etc. When Special K came out I played "I am the Walrus" by the Beatles to roars of laughter from the 800 or so lads in the room. When Brains came out he had his mate Terry holding the Fray Bentos heavyweight belt in the air with him shadow boxing behind. Their entrance music was Eye of the Tiger from the Rocky film, but half way to the ring I changed it to "Y.M.C.A." and everyone was in stitches laughing.

The fight was top notch and some big punches were thrown and the crowd was roaring both fighters on right up to the third round. By this time they were both absolutely goosed and gagging for their breath. Special K won by a unanimous points decision and held the belt in the air to roars of cheers from the crowd.

At the end of the whole day we raised £450 for each lad locked up, and over £500 for Kershaw's school for the Blind thanks to

Don Price taking a bucket round. The day went better than we ever could have imagined and people still ask me nowadays to do another one...who knows? One thing I do remember was when the police came in for a chat with me and Mickey Francis, they just looked at the boxing ring in disbelief and went to us "What is it next week..Darts!!"

Some people say to me why it has always got to be you and certain others who organise these events and be the centre of attention, and seriously think that we do it to take a slice of the money. This really makes me angry for two reasons...

1. because the person or persons, who usually asks these questions have never stepped up to help or do an event that everyone else could attend. We would be more than happy to attend similar events, but everyone knows apart from a few meet-ups in local boozers nothing ever gets done and I and a few others won't just sit back and watch our mates rot in jail or suffer from illness.

2. because frankly we don't do things for money, and never have. Anyone will tell you who has organised similar events how time consuming it is, but you know that when you decide to organise it! It's too easy for people to snipe from the outside when they don't lift a finger themselves and just sit and watch and judge others. It's a good job everyone in life doesn't do that!

The most important thing from those events we organised was that the people who they were intended to benefit received the benefit in full. We don't do it for thanks or attention; we just do it for a smile and to remind our mates whether they are in jail or struggling with illness, that if you are a city lad we don't forget you and we try our best to help you.

We'd do it for anyone of them and even for the snipers, and deep down they know that. Call us whatever you want, but I know our real mates know that's the truth.

Over the years I've grown up and had a family and realised there is more to my life than fighting at the match. I've got bigger priorities in my life, as have many lads my age that I travelled home and away with throughout the years. I may now only see them once a blue moon but I will never ever forget that part of my life and the lifelong friends I have gained.

Before I had my daughter I did not really worry about my life and nothing really scared me, but now the first thing that comes in my mind when I am in one of those situations is my kids. Sometimes you cannot walk away and have to fight, because people will see that as weakness and play you on it in your mind. Sometimes you have a choice, and my choice nowadays at 37 years old is to walk away.

I recently nearly lost a very good friend through a battle at the match, he was hit on the head with a wheel brace. The force was that much that it smashed his scull into fragments that were pushed into his brain. He had clots on his brain and the doctors lost him once which put his family through hell and back. A friend of mine was at the hospital when these events occurred and he told me it was the most harrowing scene he had ever witnessed. The patients son and his wife were screaming and crying in the waiting area thinking they were going to lose their father, husband and idol.

"Why my dad...Why my dad....I don't want to lose him" were the screams from the lads son.

All this was over rivalries over a football match between two local teams, and it's something that changed me forever. Luckily the lad recovered but carries the biggest scar on his head you have ever seen. He has plates in his head and will probably be in recovery for many a year to come. He was lucky, others situations have led to loss of life such as the young lad in Burnley after the Nottingham Forest game. He bled to death after being bottled outside a city centre bar after a fight between both sets of lads.

Another incident was when a young Manchester United fan died after a similar incident at their game away to Southampton a few years back. I often think of the awful emotional stress that those lads' parents and loved ones would have gone through when they heard the news that they had lost their son. Can you imagine the heartbreak they feel at losing their child over a game of football?

It's taken the birth of my daughter to realise how much I cherish my life and respect other people's lives. I often think about the other side of the coin as well, what the parents and families of the perpetrators have to go through when they are found guilty in court and receive heavy sentences taking huge chunks of freedom from their lives.

Yes you can say they deserve it, but usually it's their wives, girlfriend's families and kids who also pay the price more than anyone. After 20 years of following City with "Guvnors" you may say I am a hypocrite, but let me tell you one thing, we never used knives, bats, wheel braces or any other type of weapon except our fists and our heads. We never kicked anyone on the floor, and never sniped smaller groups, which we considered bullying.

One instance of this is when we played United once at COMS, and after the match we walked through an estate in Beswick near the ground about 40 handed. Next thing about 7 Men In Black (Uniteds firm) walked round the corner and their faces turned white. We all knew exactly who they were some by name and the rest by face. Rather than do the old bully trick we just made sure they knew that we knew who they were and let them walk through us. A few of the younger lads were baffled by it, but in the older lads eyes what sort of result would that have been?

Sadly nowadays a lot of so called football firms are using different tactics and different methods and taking it to the extremes of carrying knives and going tooled up. I cringe when I see these so called hooligan DVD's with packs of lads attacking the two or three lads who stood and didn't run. If that were City's lads doing that I would cringe with embarrassment. It's a cowards trick end of, and I have more respect for the lads who got clobbered rather than a pack of dogs who are throwing digs at an easy target.

The lads I went to city with over the years only fought lads who wanted to fight us, we never used tools and no innocent bystander ever copped for anything. Any lad who says he has never "Ran" is either a liar or has not been travelling or going long enough. Any firm on any given day in this country can do any other firm no matter what their reputation. Whether it is Wigan, Millwall, Lincoln, Leeds or even Accrington Stanley! Trust me City did 3 divisions in 3 years and we went everywhere and we got a few surprises.

In the past few years the whole scene is virtually dead and the life span of a football hooligan is about two years if he's lucky. Police have infiltrated most major football firms in the country with banning orders and association banning orders. If you are walking in a group of more than 3 people in the street nowadays you can get nicked as a threat to society and public order! I've spoken to a lot of lads from firms all over the country and they all say the same thing "It's had its day". Amazingly though young groups of lads are still popping up creating new firms, but the life span of them is barely lasting 12 months. Police just see the signs of a new breed, note the faces and ban them within 12 months. This way they are constantly keeping a lid on the situation and after 30 years of trying have finally contained the problem.

Like I said the Police and courts and the clubs are coming down on them like a ton of bricks and as soon as they blink they are getting banning orders and frog marched all over.

I can relate so much to lads at that age (under 21) and the way they look at the football scene, but to be honest I know there's nothing anyone can say to stop them going and getting involved, because at that age I wasn't going to listen to anyone either. The only thing that stopped me going was my family and substituting it with amateur football.

That's not the solution for everyone and I am not the one to ask on that subject. I can just write these words and let you be the judge of that, but if you are a young lad that wants to get in on the back end of the scene expect to do jail in this day and age and I mean a heavy sentence.

The Stone Island and C.P hooligan uniform used to amuse me that many football lads all over the country wore. The Stone Island badge had a target usually on the arm of any of its garments and it might as well have said "Look at me I'm a hooligan".

Now if you were a police sergeant in a morning briefing with your unit, what do you think your first instructions would be??

"Right lads, anyone with Stone Island, C.P. Company or Burberry coats I want you to follow and stop and search them" or something on those lines!

The rags firm were even worse! They all wore black and stood out like a sore thumb and were easy to identify at many City v United matches. Black jeans, black coats, black hats, black gloves.

A lot of our firm were wise to how the police had worked out how to identify lads easily and many a game we would just mix in with the straight going football fan and slip the net of the police. Some of the younger lads would constantly get pulled and I used to try and preach to them that the Stone Island badges were the problem. Now I look back I cannot believe how fast the days and the games went by and how many funny but dangerous days out we had.

In the late 90's I mainly attended games with City's notorious "Young Firm". These were in my eyes the reason City had a good firm in that era and from 1998 to 2007 they were at the forefront of every major battle we had. Walshy, Ste O'Connor, Val, Big K, Craig, Twins, Fairy, Eddie D, Tate brothers, Cliff and Dave from Wythenshawe, Danials, Burnsy, Terry, Kells, Derbo, Reidy, Eoin, Fairy etc etc. These were all good lads and people who I trusted with my life and have a top laugh with. There were probably a good 80 of us in total but too many to name.

Over the years it has saddened me to see how we have all separated and gone our different ways as many of us have got kids and families now but hey that's part of growing up and I know it is a blessing in disguise. Many people frown upon the football scene but it was no different to the Teddy boy era of the 50's, the mods and rockers of the 60's and also the skinheads and punks of the 70's and 80's. All those scenes entertained young men who participated in violence and having a laugh usually at someone's expense. The young men of those generations have silently moved on to become rocks of our societies and that is a fact. I speak a lot to men from the Manchester areas in good work positions and you would not believe some of the skeletons they have in their closets!

Again its sounds like I am endorsing football violence and football gangs, I am not, I am just accepting it was a part of my life, past tense and something I have learnt many a lesson from. Now I would never encourage this to any young lad because the easiest way to learn these things is out of books and by listening to your piers and people who have risen above taking this route and succeeded in their own lives.

Ask any football hooligan what he has lost from being involved in the scene and I will guarantee he will tell you he has lost a girlfriend, major amounts of money, freedom, jobs, family etc etc. The same as your teddy boys, punks and mods from other generations.

I have many happy memories following city and travelling the country with the guvnors of Manchester City. Much the same reply would come off a 50 year old man of today's world who was a scooter boy, mod or teddy boy of the 1960's. People may frown upon that comment but I can't try and hide my past, that's not the sort of person I am. What's done is done and none of us should look back on our lives and regret it to a degree where it haunts us. Life is about learning from your mistakes and making sure you do not repeat them by progressing without hurting or damaging anyone else while on your journey.

Following football was not a mistake in my eyes, it was and still is something I love. No, I wouldn't go around cracking people because of the team I or they support anymore. I have learnt that we are all the same on this planet and we all have more in common than meets the eye.

Sometimes I think deeply about why me like any other football lad wanted to fight over a game of football played by players who just played for the love of the game. I have many great friends and relatives who are United, Oldham, Everton, Liverpool, Leeds and Stockport fans and I often think of how I would feel if they got injured or attacked at a football match. I got away lightly over the years with a few court cases and a banning order and a few light sentences in jail and A.C

A.C. was a term for attendance centre that was set up in the 80's to prevent young men from attending football matches once they had been found guilty of football related offences. It was usually held facing the BBC studios on Oxford road in Manchester on a Saturday afternoon. It was run by prison officers and the government used it as a sort of 4 hour boot camp.

I first attended in the 1980's when I was banned from the match for fighting at a Chelsea game on the forecourt at Maine Road. On my first arrival I was ten minutes late as I struggled to find the place. As soon as I walked through the door I was asked my name and given a number. As soon as I was booked in, the screw (prison officer) told me to give him 50.

I just looked at him and said "50 what??"

He slapped me round the head and said "50 press ups dickhead"

I swear I just wanted to walk out then but I had heard that if you did you were given a custodial sentenced when you went back to court.

After doing 50 press ups I was sweating cobs and he lifted me by my 10 stone frame and through me down the corridor through some swinging doors. The room was full of young lads all aging from 16 to 21 and they all turned their heads and laughed at me while I picked myself up from the floor. Within 5 seconds the screws had 5 lads on the floor doing press ups who had been laughing. It was a pretty brutal start to my 50 hours community service but something that was an eye opener.

Once I had settled down I noticed their was a major divide of lads, I recognised a few other city lads such as "Slicker" and "Yozzer" with a few other faces I didn't know. On the other side of the room was a few of United's young firm who later went on to call themselves the young Munich's. There were a few lads from Bolton and Oldham, but they kept themselves to themselves. The screws recognised the divide and straight away mixed us up and split us into 3 classes so there was no chance of gang warfare breaking out on campus.

Over the next 11 weeks we had classes on fitness, football, teamwork, drugs, sex, prison life and everyone's favourite...First aid! Now this may surprise you but when I tell you the reason behind this you will fully understand why. We were in the classroom slouching on the chairs like a bunch of teenage rebels who were just waiting for home time looking into thin air, when one of the screws brought out an imitation dummy and placed it on the table. We were to learn how to resuscitate someone who was unconscious by giving them heart massage and mouth to mouth. The screw got our attention by asking a few questions...

"Right lads, I want to ask you what is the first thing you do when you find someone unconscious?

The class was silent with everyone totally uninterested in the discussion. All of a sudden "Slicker" my mate from Chadderton put up his hand...

"YES"......asked the screw and pointed at slicker.

'That's easy boss........see if he's got a wallet"

Well the whole classroom went up in hysterics...within 10 seconds we were all doing 50 press-ups. It took us all a good ten minutes as we were laughing that much. Once we got back to our seats the screw tried to make an example of Slicker by using him as a volunteer to copy his example of how to give heart massage and give mouth to mouth to the dummy. The screw went through the procedure and as he finished he cleaned the mouth of the dummy with some sort of cleaning agent with a tissue. As Slicker gave mouth to mouth to the dummy we were amazed as he did it perfectly. Then to our amazement he asked could he do it again as he did not feel he did it properly. He picked up the bottle of cleaning agent and wiped the mouth of the dummy with it. This time as slicker raised his head his eyes became all glazed and he started grinning like a Cheshire cat....he was wired off the chemical used to clean the mouth piece. All the lads knew it but the screw was not on to it at all. Once slicker got back to his chair he sat down and put his head in his hands laughing to himself.

"Right who thinks they can do as good as an example as Slicker?"

Every lad in the class put his hand up in the classroom and rushed to the front. Within 20 minutes 10 lads were having the giggles soaking this dummies mouth with the cleaning agent and doing mouth to mouth resuscitation with it.

In the end the screw got onto it and we were doing press ups in hysterics. Slicker was a top lad and I have not seen him for many years. Like me he got caught up in the world of drugs and stopped going to the match but I have fond memories of funny times with him and many of the other Mills Hill Villains who went to City.

Even though I show the funny side of my punishments it taught me a lot when the law punished me. I did serve a light prison sentence due to non payment of fines for violent disorder at a football match and was jailed due to me trying to make a mockery of the legal system. After violence at a City v Oldham fixture in the early 90's I was given a three hundred pound fine which I had made no attempt to pay whatsoever. I attended court dressed like a typical football lad with my mates Jason Barry and Mark O'Brien. As I stood in the dock I was questioned as to why I had made no attempt to pay it. At that time in my life I was a cocky, confident typical "scally"

"What it is your honour, I have been a short of cash recently and I have had no bus fare to get to college never mind court. I'm only on 30 quid a week as a YTS trainee and I'm totally pot less"

The three magistrates went into their chambers and came back into the court as I winked at Jay and Mark O'Brien in the courtroom. Within minutes of them returning in the court I was sentenced to 28 days and I was gob smacked as Jay and OB giggled and told me to pass them my car keys.

Prison taught me a few things about survival and how crazy some people actually are. I met a lad on my first day who was serving 4 years for biting another lad's ear off. He seemed a decent lad, but was not bothered about doing time as he said to me he could do 4 years stood on his head. I often thought about the logic of that comment and I was determined I would never return to prison.

Even though I went to AC and prison I still could not stop myself from getting involved with the lads at the match. It just made me think more at the match and as many of the wiser old heads taught us, as a firm we just became wiser and used stealth tactics to greater affect.

CHAPTER 3

"GETTING INVOLVED IN THE GAME"

As I was getting older I was getting wiser and starting to realise I would be stupid to carry on going to watch City doing what I was doing. I was getting a name for myself as one of the main lads at City. This was not because I was a hard nut or a psychopath but basically because I was now organising away coaches and meeting times for away matches. It was nothing I ever wanted to happen or had planned... it just happened.

I remember where it all started; I was sat in the Clarence pub near Maine Road with a few of the lads from the match, Jonah, Burnsy, Craig and Eddie Dolan. After a chat about away travel we decided to hire a car for an away game to Spurs. There was that much interest we ended up hiring a Mini bus for 15 of us to go and it ended up a great day out.

It was such a good day out that word got round and within a few weeks I had people hounding me to sort coaches out. After a discussion with a few of the lads I decided it was a "Go'er" and I ended up taking two coaches to Arsenal. We went to a boozer called "The Worlds End" in Camden Town and met other lads down there and we had a 200 strong mob! I remember Craig from Partington and Derbo from Moston saying to me "You've started something now". Arsenal showed with about 30 but didn't even bother putting up a fight as they weren't expecting us with such numbers. City got hammered 5-1 with Tiatto getting red carded.

Over the next few years with the help of a Blackley lad called Dryer and the "Young Firm" we travelled all over the country by coach or train. We had some great days out and some of the funniest times of my life but it was getting to the point where the hassle off the police was getting to me and a few of the others. We would constantly be getting a Section 60 (a stop and search) sometimes 3 times a game. I would be getting police officers from away grounds pulling me out with two or three others and telling me they were watching me then put me in a van for ten minutes and give me a few sly digs. This was pretty common amongst a few of the older lads as the police were starting to have a zero tolerance attitude to football so they would just look at disorganising football firms as much as they could by taking out the regular faces.

A few of us would get lads walking up to us who we didn't know and asking us where Citys firm were and what was happening. It used to do our head's in as we used to think any of these weirdo's could be a copper undercover! I would also get lads phoning me from other firms saying so and so had give them my number, and mithering me to death. It could have been MI5 for all I knew or the Old Bill!

It did my head in once when I was in town with a girl I was seeing, and some little scruffy United lad just came up to me at my table and went "see you on Derby Day Cooper….knob head!" Here I was in the Kwok Man Restaurant on a Tuesday night and some little idiot is boring me about the match in front of a girl who I am trying to hide from my football life. I just flew at him in a rage and we both went over a table, next thing I'm getting whacked with the heel of a stiletto on the back of my head off his mad Chav blond bird with big hooped earrings! She was more of a handful than the lad, and it took three waiters to get her out of the restaurant. My neck was a mess but the waiters and the girl I was with cleaned me up and I had a laugh about it later, but it certainly had an effect on my outlook on life and made me realise the hooligan tag was with me 7 days a week

.

Away from the football I was also involved in things that were having a similar effect and I was finding I was getting involved with people who were way out of my league. They were doing things I could have easily participated in, but just couldn't bring myself to do as I had a heart and believed in the old proverb "Live by the sword, die by the sword" These were international people and I was making and blowing major money and gaining a lot of enemies as well as plastic friends and plastic girlfriends.

When you mix in these circles you start to think you're invincible to the affects of drugs and I was no different. I was starting to suffer from major depression (which I hid) through splitting up and losing my long term girlfriend and was turning to cocaine more and more. It got to the point where it was affecting my attitude to work as well and I was letting people down. My whole life was on straw foundations and cocaine was giving me one step forward but three steps back. I was getting drugs laid on to pay other people off and I realised that my life was heading towards disaster. I remember I was working on some penthouse apartments in Manchester City Centre and I was using cocaine in the day with a few other lads just to feel normal. To me at that time being normal was being coked up as it made me relax and forget about the depressing things in life. Well it did for 3 or 4 hours but when I was alone at home it just made it 10 times worse.

I decided to get away from it all and go to Australia on a 12 month working visa, it was to be the best decision I ever made in my life and changed me for the better. I had organised a leaving party of just my friends and I had a meal with my family as I didn't expect to come back. I was determined to start a fresh life and just bought a one-way ticket to Oz stopping at Bangkok and Taiwan. The leaving do was attended by a lot of lads from City and also lads (and girls) who I had grown up with and loved both Reds and Blues. Funnily enough afterwards we all went to a night spot called the Amber club in Newton Heath just outside Manchester (soul club of the year in the Daily Mirror - Honest!) later on where it all kicked off with a mass fight!! What a send off???

I remember being at Manchester Airport the morning after hugging my mam, I really was adamant I wasn't coming back and had to hold back the tears. My first flight was Manchester to Dubai and I was told by one of the "jibbers" from the Parkside how to swindle it in a first class seat. He told me to just wait till everyone had boarded and when the last call came just walk through. This way I had to walk through the first class seats and if there was an empty one just sit down and fall asleep.

Happy days! I flew first class all the way (3 flights) to Sydney, in a reclining leather seat with a fold away tv and free everything. On the last leg of the journey a pretty stewardess pulled me and asked was I really supposed to be sat in first class? I told her I was a Manc and "all Mancs were first class luv!" She just smiled and said thanks for flying China Airlines. To which I replied "The pleasure was all mine".

I stayed in the Northern Beaches part of Sydney, in a place called Harbord just next to Manly. Luckily for me Harbord had a few ex-pats from my home town Failsworth who I had been at school with, Graham Davidson, Kenny Williams, Allan Jackson, Lee Palmer, Heath Donnelly and Neville Taylor had all created a mini Failsworth community in Manly and all at one point or another looked after me.

Australia was the first place I had ever felt racially intimidated and it opened up my eyes into how other people have to cope with this issue. After 3 weeks I could not get work anywhere and I was a qualified plumber. As soon as I said I was English people would hang up the phone or just say they were not interested. Neville used to say a lot of Aussies hated the "Poms" but if you had an Irish second name you would get work as there was a bigger affinity to the Irish? Luckily a lad called Heath Donnelly gave me work window cleaning on his round doing the skyscrapers in Sydney in cradles hanging over the side. It was a great job but I would get a tanned back with a white front and look like a jaffa-cake at the end of the day.

While I was in Australia I stopped drinking and smoking and also started getting fit again. I also started to go to The Church Of Jesus Christ Of Latter Day Saints in Harbord where I met some Tongan lads called Maffu and Jordan who were only young, but huge in stature. They were bang into their weights and kept me focused on workouts.

They also got me a job on New Years Eve at a club called "The Cave" in Star City which is in Sydney. The club was a local haunt for all the local celebs like the Minnogue sisters and the boxer Mundaine, as well as big TV stars. It was also a local meet up for Sydney's biggest criminals from the underworld of the Lebanese. I was to work the door with the lads doing security, which really did not appeal to me at all. I was 14 stone and the only white man on display and a dwarf to all the other doormen there who all looked like WWF wrestlers. At first I got a few stares but after a while loads of the doormen and other people who I didn't know were coming up to me and shaking my hand introducing themselves for no reason whatsoever. Then girls were hitting on me asking for my number! It all seemed too weird and I noticed Maffu and Jordan were constantly smiling at me.

"What you two laughing at...Come on tell me?" I said.

It later became aware to me that they had told everyone I was an ex SAS soldier and was a new starter. When I found out I was relieved, and played along with it for a good few weeks and got a good few perks out of it. There were a few fights but nothing major, and nine times out of ten it was girls fighting so we just picked them up and launched them.

All the doorman at the club were either Maori, Tongan or Polynesian and belonged to a religion, and it hit home to me how none of them were scared of death. They would front gangs of 50 "Lebs" with knives, guns, the lot outside and not even wear vests. They would say to me...

"Cooper! Death is just a passage to another life and if you have faith you have led a good life on earth, you will get to that next life"

They say that "Islanders" or coconuts as they call themselves, have bones twice as thick as any other race and I honestly say I have never met harder or stronger lads who can fight in my life. Their secret is a natural steroid they eat called "Taro" which is basically a sweet potato. I reckon if you had 10 of this lot in a football firm you would have done everyone!

If you ever get chance to go to Manly in Sydney, go to the Stain pub near the front and check the doormen out. If you sit outside on a Friday night you will see them deal with loads of gobby backpackers giving it the "biggun". They just slap them and don't even punch them, as they know they could kill them. As time went by in Oz I did become homesick. City were flying under Kevin Keegan and I would often think of my family and how they were coping with life back home. I still didn't know if I wanted to stay and start a new life or return to England. Australia was the most beautiful place I have ever lived in. The country's government spends more on sports than its defence, and there is so much for kids to do. I didn't meet one family whose kids were not involved in football, rugby, cricket, gym, surfing, swimming, diving, water-skiing, fishing, or volleyball. The place was overflowing with stuff for kids to do, football pitches and rugby pitches were everywhere and every member of a family was involved in either the organisation or participation. The biggest thing for me was they welcomed everyone no matter how good you were or where you were from. In the northern beaches all the kids always looked healthy and you rarely saw a fat kid or fat family. The place was a great community and there was something for everyone. No threatening gangs of kids hanging about at night on the streets and if you did see some they were usually polite and moved aside for you.

It was a template that communities and councils in this country should use as a blueprint to bring down these tribal conflicts that are taking our kids lives in this country.

My final decision on whether to stay or return was decided by a Glasgow Rangers fan. I cannot remember his name but he had been in Oz since he was 16 and now had 4 kids and was 42 years of age. I asked him had he regretted settling in Oz and did he get homesick. This was basically his reply that sticks in my head till this day.

"Glasgow, when I left was a poor city, there was only two ways out and that was in a coffin or by foot. As soon as I arrived in Oz I saw the land and met the people and knew in my heart I would be stupid to go back to the grey city. I was running away from my birthplace that I loved, but knew it could never give me in a lifetime, a tenth of what Sydney had to offer in a minute. I have been here while my mother and father have died as well as a brother, and that broke my heart and I have never had the money to visit their graves. I spoke to them constantly before they died and they told me they were proud of me and I did the right thing and the best for my family and their name. Although deep down I still live with the pain of not being there for them, my family here compensates it."

I realised from that day, how much my family (and my mates) meant to me. There was no way I could be on the other side of the world if anyone was ill or had died. It would kill my heart and my soul and I couldn't live a happy life.   I would sit on Manly beach watching kids play beach football with the sun setting in the background listening to the Happy Mondays on my Walkman. I would constantly think about ways I could live my life without getting involved in crime and drugs and maybe putting a bit back into the community and the game of football I had taken for granted. To tell the truth the answers did not come at that moment but I knew God had made me a Mancunian for a reason, and there was no point of running away from it.

Within a week I'd said my farewells to my friends and Davo, James Gorman and Kenny Williams took me to the airport. Funnily enough I had my first beer for 9 months to celebrate and one thing that sticks in my mind was my cases were stopped from going on the plane for being over weight for the return journey! Kenny my friend ended up copping for loads of my Armani and Paul and Shark jeans (which he still wears today!!) haha

After 26 hours of flying I got off the plane at Manchester airport, it was chucking it down, I just stood in the rain and looked at the grey sky for 2 minutes to realise I loved the place and it was my home. MANCHESTER!

(Many people hate rain, but I love it and always have. I can walk in it for hours - maybe it's a Mancunian thing I don't know?)

After a month home I bumped into an old school friend called Amanda Edwards who I had basically grown up with. I had always liked Amanda, but life had dictated that we weren't to be. If I were single she would be with someone, and if she were single I would be with someone. We never spoke about it until we were together but maybe that was how it was just meant to be. I was informed that she had been split up from her boyfriend and was single. I couldn't believe it and as soon as we met I asked her for out for a drink. Anyway, wham, bam thank you mam.. a month later we're together and she is pregnant and I'm settling down - house the lot, but with complacency I was slowly drifting back into the City syndrome getting up to my old tricks.

As most of you know a pregnant woman's hormones go up in the air when they are "tubbed", and Amanda was no different. She'd go ballistic arguing and crying telling me not to go to the match as I had responsibilities and she did not want a father of her baby in jail or maimed.

We sat down and discussed it in depth and I realised I had to substitute going to the match with the lads with something else. First we tried family shopping on a match day, which consisted of us going to the Trafford Centre or the Arndale looking in 30 baby shops or women's clothes shops.

As all men know it is a nightmare!! "Do you like this?, What do you think of this? Can we afford this? WERE YOU LOOKING AT THAT GIRLS ARSE THEN??"

Sometimes I would connect my headphones to a radio to try and listen to the match as we went shopping. In the end we would be at each other's throats and it would end up in tears at home. I would come home with clothes and she would come home with nothing which would always baffle her??

I was starting to realise that women have to go in 30 shops whereas us men can go in 1 or 2 and buy something. This was something I was never going to get used to... Simple....I had to find a hobby!

It was by chance I was in a pub called the Royal Oak in Failsworth one Sunday when I met a local young lad called Stephen Scullion. I was informed that he was a young United lad who was running a pub team called "Marina FC" in the Ashton Sunday League. We got talking about it and he asked me if I fancied helping out, it didn't take me long to respond and on the Thursday I met the team at Ten Acres Lane in Newton Heath for training.

The team was made up of a bunch of young lads ranging from 17 to 19 who had only won one game all season. Scully was only 19 himself and they treated him more like a mate than a manager so there was no leadership whatsoever. At the first session I could see there were some decent players and it seemed a great challenge to get the team fixed. Gally was a lad who played wide right, a tricky winger from Newton Heath but very light in build. Phil Army was a good all round footballer who I could see had lungs of a lion and the build of a gazelle. Teazer, Platty, Starkie and John Elliott all had good ability but different strengths and weaknesses. I knew then, with a few more players added I had the ingredients of a decent team that could do something, but most of all the thing that drove me to manage them was they all wanted to win, succeed and enjoy it.

I became manager with Scully as my number 2 with just 3 games to go. We drew 1, lost 1 and won 1. I just upped the fitness training and moved people about in different positions where I thought they would be stronger. At the end of the season we were all confident that we could give it a real go and do something the next year. I was like a dog with a new bone and was determined to do everything to be a success. As I was attending league meetings it was frightening me to death of how costly running a football team was:

£400 for the pitch

£75 League Registration

£8 booking

£35 Sending off

£25 an hour for training on the astro turf

£35 Insurance (that only pays out for Broken bones not ligaments??)

The Marina pub at this time was being run by two women who were dizzy as anything and I hated the pub. When we used to go in for the football nets on a Sunday the dog which was a Pitbull had usually urinated all over them and we would have to put them up with shirts over our noses to stop breathing in the stench.

The box that stored the subs went missing and financially we were on our backsides. After a short meeting Scully and me decided to take a new sponsorship offer up from another landlord called Chris at The Pack Horse in Failsworth. He bought us a kit and paid our pitch fees for the new season and it was a big weight off our finances so things were easy from then on. We got in some great players from other teams that had folded in the area.

Andrew Wolfe was a great centre half and great talker and looking back was our version of the Man United and Aston Villa legend Paul McGrath. Wolfy did not have the quickest feet but he made up for it with his brains and his leadership skills. He was a lazy trainer but someone who added vast experience at the back.

Matt Grandon was a goal machine from Miles Platting who could make a goal and score from anywhere. He was your Sunday League version of Thierry Henri. We had another great lad called Paul Renshaw who was a lookalike for the Italian player who was at Sampdoria called Lombardo.

Craig Reid was a quality centre half; he played at United and City as a kid, but could explode at anytime and was today's modern version of Vinnie Jones. He looked like Vinnie now I come to think of it, and he certainly had more tattoo's.

Ryan Boardman was a pacey midfielder who scored great goals and was just full of energy and running. He was Ex-Army and was a lad who you needed with discipline and heart.

Zac Macela was a young 16 year old lad who played like a man twice his age. Zac was young at the time but came from a good family with good morals and a never say die attitude. All the older lads looked after him but we soon realised he could look after himself as his father had taught him how to balance his discipline to be a winner and not a sinner.

Craig Bezzina was a goalkeeper with Italian family from Limeside which is a tough council estate in Oldham. Craig was a quality keeper but liked a smoke before and after the game which made his reactions slower. He was a great keeper but now and again would make a costly mistake due to his head being in the clouds (usually of smoke). I would often shout at him to put his cig out during the middle of a match or at half time!

The Mrs (Amanda) was more than happy that I was involved in amateur football rather than me going to watch City, as she knew I couldn't spend all my money and get nicked on a field watching 22 lads playing football. Also, I was now the proud father of Millie Rose Cooper as well as my stepdaughter Cherelle and my priorities were with my family for the first time in my life. They relied on me to be an example and a father in everything I did

With Sky TV growing, more and more football was available to watch on the box and I was saving a fortune just doing the pub terrace rather than the football terrace. I was also going to bed early on a Saturday night because I had a big amateur game on the Sunday. Some nights Amanda would have 15 shirts hanging on radiators drying for the game the next day, but she would rather have that as a job than phoning me to see what part of the country I was in and if I was in trouble and in one piece.

The start of the next season saw City in the Premiership and The Pack Horse in the Ashton Sunday League Division 1. Keegan had got City promoted and Scully and me had got the Pack Horse promoted by applying for a higher division. Luckily they merged two divisions into one and we were all made up. With our new navy blue and orange kit we looked the part and we even played good football. We were simply outplaying teams with our finishing and fitness levels. Our two strikers Matt Grandon and Phil Army were bagging goal after goal and even the wingers Teazer and Gally were chipping in with a few. Houghton (Strength), Boardy (Pace) and Smell (heart) were just the best mixture ever in midfield. At the back Reidy, Starkie, Wolfy and Platty's back four had kept 9 consecutive clean sheets which pushed us way up the league.

We got to the semi-finals of the cup, and were in a two horse race for the league title. Due to our pitch being bad in winter we had three games in hand on the Lark who were from Hollinwood. They were top, 7 points clear of us with Queen Anne "B" from Shaw in second. All we had to do was win our 3 games in hand, which seemed more than achievable as we had beat all the opposition in the other games. Our first game was against the Queen Anne "B" away in Oldham on a Wednesday night. I couldn't make it due to a meeting with a few of the lads from city who were making a CD in a recording studio, so I left it in the capable hands of Scully.

We had beat the Queen Anne "B" 8-1 in the home fixture, but word was out they were putting ringers in as they didn't want a manc team winning the league. I was still confident we would win convincingly and left the lads to it. At 7:30pm I get a call of Scully saying the match had been abandoned because of fighting. Apparently the Queen Anne had put their A Team in and they were beating us 2-1, the referee was letting bad tackles go and all hell had broke loose. Reidy, who wasn't playing saw one of their players punch ours on the back of the head and ran on to drag him off. Then 2 more spectators ran on from the oppositions side and it was a 15 minute free for all punch up. Scully told me later that the other team were just constantly winding the lads up and the referee lost the plot and was not protecting our players, to which they just snapped. It was a ploy that annoyed me even more when I found out that their secretary was on the Leagues Committee.

On the Monday I had a phone call saying we were suspended from the league until a meeting and then an FA hearing. They knew that there was no way we could get a hearing before the end of the season and basically through us to the dogs. I felt physically sick and I was determined to fight the league all the way to clear our name. The lads were absolutely devastated and I felt more for them than anything else.

The league made a decision without a hearing, without witnesses and without and appeal. I took the matter to the Manchester County FA where I proved we were innocent. A member of the League Committee had doctored a date on a letter for an appeal from me and said it was late, but failed to read the content of the letter which proved the date it was sent. I will never forget to this day the look on the league committee's faces when they were told they were in the wrong and not us.

Me and Scully were laughing or heads off in the car park at Brantingham Road, We, "Pack Horse FC" were totally cleared and I'm led to believe the Ashton Sunday League received a heavy fine for their misconduct in this matter. What ticked me off was we did not get compensated for the loss of our season or our chance of trophies. All that season had been for nothing, and the only benefactor was the FA receiving its fine money from the league, which I believe was a 3 figure sum.

The next season we would have to move pubs yet again as word had it Chris the landlord of the Pack Horse was doing a moonlight. I got wind of this and went round to the pub to get the kit as it was our pride and joy. All the curtains were shut and it had been closed for 3 days with no sign of life, so I decided to kick the door in. The place stunk! All the fridges still had beer in but there was food everywhere and it looked like someone was in a rush to get off. I got in the kitchen and found all the football gear and put it in my car. I decided to cover my arse so I contacted the brewery and told them the script, as Chris had robbed our football subs and me and Scully wanted to kill him.

To my amazement, they asked me to look after the pub for a few days and said I could have any stock that was left in the fridges. I was straight on the phone and within minutes my mates Darren Beswick and Aki came round with a lad called McFad. They walked in and I just sat behind the bar and said

"What's yours?" to which they all just screamed laughing.

We got hammered and with the help of the Pinder brothers we had a real drink in a pub where we were landlords for a day! (not before tidying the pub up which was left in a rotten state). Two days later the pub was dry and we handed it back to the brewery.

By now I was sick of pub landlords and all their promises, but I decided to give a pub one last go. It was a boozer with a stable landlord and a good reputation for football. The 8 Bells is situated on Alder Road in Failsworth, and the landlord Scottish Robbie took no shit and had been there for years and me and Scully were convinced it could work - we were wrong! 2 months after the season kicked off Robbie had a slight health problem and sold out to a local councillor called Howard who was not interested in a pub team, no food after the game just a few Lucozades and we were off.

As the 8 bells FC we went into the Tameside League Division 1 competing with teams such as Newton Heath Loco "A" Newton Heath Loco "B" White Horse, Angel Riverside and The Gardeners (Droylsden). These were the main contenders for the title and teams in the league mainly came from areas in Manchester such as Droylsden, Gorton, Beswick, Openshaw, Abbey Hey. As well as Tameside teams from Dukinfield Ashton and Reddish. The standard was a lot higher than the Ashton Sunday League but we did well with additions such as Alex Dodd and Ryan Shaunnessy (aged just 16). Doddy was a combative player and a total powerhouse with the ball and could shoot from anywhere. Shaunno was a lad I spotted playing for Failsworth Dynamo's and was a pacey left footed winger full of tricks, flicks and turns. A lot of the lads doubted me signing him but he changed our season and proved my judgement by scoring a 25 yard volley on his debut.

I was and still am a big believer in rotating teams as players rotate football around their social lives, so why can't the manager rotate players round the games. The White Horse were running away with the league by not losing a game as well as just conceding 3, and Lee Bowles Newton Heath Loco's were running away with second spot.

We managed to go on a run in the league cup, and played the semi-finals on Mellands against Angel Riverside and were losing 2-1 with 3 minutes to go. We hit the bar, the upright and it just did not look like we would score. Then with a minute to go Dave Starkie hit a rasper that the keeper tipped over the bar for a corner. If I remember rightly Teaser took a poor corner from the right and "Lombardo" Renshaw headed the ball in the goal about a foot off the ground. It was the scrappiest goal you ever saw. We all just went mental and ran on the pitch jumping all over each other. The feeling of joy and relief was so good we might as well have been at Wembley rather than Mellands. As a manager I was trying to calm down to get the players heads switched on, as I knew 30 minutes of extra time was looming. Me and Scully looked at the players of the Angel Riverside and they were gone, exhausted and mentally drained. I knew we were in our first final in my heart, but my head told me to bring the lads back down to earth and get the job done. We scored 2 more goals in extra time and the celebrations were something that will stay with me for the rest of my life. Ever since I was a kid I had never been in a final watching City, playing for the school or even Failsworth Tigers. It was a personal milestone in my life and really did a lot for me and I learnt so much from the experience I can't put it into words. Eighteen months previous, 7 of these lads were in a team that was bottom of the Ashton Sunday League Division 3. The same lads were now in a final at Ashton Uniteds' ground in the month of April BUZZZZZZINNNNG.

We were to play the White Horse who had by this time won the league and were unbeaten in the whole season only conceding 4 goals, but had only beaten us 1-0 and drawn with us 1-1. All of a sudden we had training and players turned up out of the woodwork wanting a place in the final.

I sat down with Scully debating who should play in the final, and funnily enough it wasn't the strongest team, but the team of the lads who had been there through thick and thin and not let us down. Looking back I went with my heart and not my head, but that's the way I've been brought up. It was one of the hardest things I had to do naming that team, but in my heart it was the easiest. I named a squad of 15 which left a few players out. Scully booked a coach with tinted windows to give it "The Real Deal" feel. We met at the Star Inn pub and the lads were buzzing at the transport we laid on. I bought loads of Lucozade Sports drinks and new balls. I wanted to make everyone of them feel special so it was like their FA Cup Final (it was in my eyes as I was a blue!)

We had a brief team talk in the function room of the pub, it had a stage, so me a Scully used it so we could get their total attention. I did one of my Winston Churchill speeches (ask former players) telling the lads we were underdogs and had nothing to lose. I told them how proud I was of them and how proud they should be of each other and that if we worked as a team like we did in the semi-final and not as individuals we would beat any team in the league. I really believed what I said and I know the players believed it after that speech, because when they walked out they were all totally silent.

We arrived at the ground very early and we had a good warm up, which was a religion of mine even during my Sunday League days. Some Sunday teams would look at us like aliens because we would warm up 20 minutes before kick off and it sent a message that we were serious in what we were doing. The first team I ever saw do it on a Sunday was Bruno's (Phil Brown) Failsworth Grey Horse, the current North West Sunday League Champions of Champions. He treats his amateur players like pro's and gets the same response back off his players in the way they play and the way they talk to him. He gives them the best kit, the best pitch and the best balls and most of all, the best preparation. The blokes won over 30 trophies in 25 years so he must be doing something right? He's become a great friend I have learnt a hell of a lot off him and still ask him for advice now.

After the warm up the players went into the dressing room and I remember a member of the league committee shaking my hand at the tunnel.

 "Good Luck Simon...you will have your work cut out today, I doubt you will get a result but hey who knows?"

He probably didn't realise what he said, but I was livid and I steamed in to the dressing room and slammed the door. I grabbed each player independently and told them their role as I named the team. Any manager will tell you the hardest decision is naming a Cup Final Team, and today mine was naming a lad called Kyle Pollit as sub. Kyle was a quiet lad but hard as nails and you just didn't want to upset him. I had to pull him to the side and told him in the tunnel, he looked at me and I swear steam came out of his ears, He was fuming but didn't argue as he knew deep down I couldn't drop the other centre half Platty as he had been there all season. Kyle was probably a better player but Platty and Wolfy were forming a good defensive partnership and I didn't want to disrupt it. As I said before my heart ruled my head and that's me, take it or leave it and I am not ever going to change. I also put Phil Army who was a utility man, on the right as I knew we needed a tackler there rather than an offensive winger as they had a good left-winger who I knew was their main threat. Young 16 year old Ryan Shaunnessy was on the left and he would prove to be too much for the White Horse. They were a bigger, more physical team than us and had a lad called Billy who was good in the air, I stressed to the lads how important it was to pass the ball on the floor when we had it and not let the White Horse get the ball to Billy, and use the width of the pitch with wing play pulling their back four wide open for Matty G and Boardy. When we didn't have the ball I insisted we closed down very quickly with tight marking supporting the constant closing down the rest of the team did so that their players would make mistakes and give us possession back.

For the first time in my management life they actually listened to me. Within 20 minutes we were 2-0 up with goals from Matty Grandon and Boardy and Scully was running up and down the line like a mad man. We got to half time and I just told the players to go out and do the same with the same commitment and passion. Within 15 minutes we scored another 2 from the goal machine Matty Grandon and were 4-0 up against the League Champions. I made changes to give the subs their chance and we just ran the show from start to finish. Wolfy, Platty and Elliot were just class at the back and Shaunnessy was megging their right back and doing "o lays" to the amusement of the crowd. The whistle blew and we just all went mental, I ran over to Doddy who was unreal in midfield and just said thanks, he had covered every blade of grass as had Phil Army.

By rights on paper we shouldn't have won that game, but looking back we deserved to because some of the players went on to become great amateur players for teams like The Grey Horse and Avro's and really they were just a bunch of lads with different qualities that gelled into a good team. They weren't the best Sunday League team, far from it...but they were a team and a winning team that beat the odds and that's what made the moment great.   I was informed the attendance was one of the highest in the leagues history and numbered 450 plus. We got back to the pub and just filled the trophy with a mixture of every drink you can think of and passed it round till we were ruined until 3 in the morning.

Stenny the red, who's one of my best mates, was given the task of filming the final with Scully's camcorder. Sadly when we played it at home it showed ten minutes and the camera all of a sudden then falls into Stenny's crotch. He only fell asleep as he was wrecked out of his head. I was gutted but now find it pretty funny as Stenny was the last person we should have picked. He had more chemicals and alcohol running through him than ICI and the Budweiser Brewery put together that night!

Matt Grandon got player of the season after scoring an incredible 42 goals, he also got top scorer and player's player. Without doubt the best striker running with the ball I have ever seen in Sunday League. His finishing was second to none, and he was just one of many great football players from the Ancoats, Miles Platting area I was to meet over the next few years.

Winning that final was one of my greatest personal achievements in my life. It was not about the trophy now I look back. It was about the fact that 16 lads had come together from nowhere and from all different backgrounds and different lives and families and areas. We had all worked under one name in wind hail and snow for 2 years and built up new friendships which had broken barriers and built bridges between us for life. We had overcome the odds of beating a team that had not been beaten all season. The manner in which we did it made me emotional as it was flowing football and we did not just beat them we played them off the park. It taught me that if you work hard together as team and show respect and loyalty to each other no matter what your age, you can achieve what everyone else thinks is impossible.

Yes it was only a divisional cup in the Tameside Second Division, but it might as well of been Wembley to me and the players due to the fact that we had done it together. It was a mixture of lads with all different qualities and all different weaknesses that had created a formula to win against the odds. It is something that has taught me and the players a huge lesson in life, and something we will carry and cherish forever.

Football is a powerful tool that can have such a huge impact on lives and is something that many of us take for granted. I dream one day of working in the football industry purely for this reason, and that's what makes me determined now at the age of 37 to get as educated as I can to achieve that dream. I will always be involved at an amateur level but my aim is to reach for the stars.

In today's football climate the odds are against me achieving that but you don't progress if you do not face adversity.

CHAPTER 4

"FOOTBALL'S LOSING IT'S ROOTS!"

As I became more and more involved in amateur football I started to watch professional football in a different way. I would watch player's positions and their movement off the ball and how they drew defenders out of play with passing movements. I started reading coaching books and autobiographies by famous players and managers, and was besotted by the whole thing. I was studying how a local guy called Phil Brown ran his outfit "The Grey Horse F.C" and would speak to his players on a weekly basis.

Over that summer in 2002 I organised a summer football tournament for all the Sunday teams in Failsworth and called it The "Billy Grogan" Failsworth Cup. I had never done this sort of thing before and not a lot of people ever believed I could pull it off. I wrote to 10 teams and after great feedback we had two groups of five teams sorted to start in July.

The following part of this chapter may talk about people and areas you have never heard of, but some of the situations and characters I mention may have relevance to your own experiences in football.

The Failsworth Cup used to be a traditional competition in our area and all the games were regularly well attended, sometimes up to 100 people would attend and players would be flocking to play in it.

I decided to name it in respect of a great pal of mine called Billy Grogan. Billy's a lovely little Irish fella, and was *apparently* a great player in his day. He has run pub teams for years in Failsworth, mostly from the Bricklayers Arms or the Guido. He was also involved in the original Failsworth Town and just recently has built a new kids club called Failsworth West. He's nearly 70 years of age and in my eyes is an icon in more ways than one. With the help of Mrs Littlewood the two have created and maintained a great club.

(I was annoyed to find out that Failsworth was having a statue of Ben Brierley put on the pole in remembrance of his great poetry. In my eyes it should be people like Billy Grogan who get statues put up, these are the people that are the heart of a community and make it beat. I don't know anyone from Failsworth who has read any of Mr Brierley's stuff and to me it was a complete waste of taxpayer's money. Read further on......)

Players were each charged £10 to play in the competition with all the money that was raised going to local kids football teams. I was shocked when the council charged me £780 for the hire of two public grass pitches on Mable Road and Brierley Avenue for just two weeks of football especially when all the money raised was going to local teams! With a total of 20 matches everyone was really excited and it was like having the Champions League of Sunday League football in the summer. Local teams Failsworth Athletic, Failsworth Dynamos, Guido FC, Warwick United, Railway Newton Heath, The Britannia, Newton Heath Loco's, The Grey Horse, Moston Villa were just some of the teams that entered the competition over the two years I did it and it was a real success with some great football.

The first year of the Failsworth Cup, Scully and me had merged with a kids team called Mable Athletic and had re-formed as Failsworth Town FC. Two good friends called Pat Dillon and Alan McKewan ran the under 12's and we ran the seniors. We were sick of relying on pub landlords who were constantly lying to us and decided to become an independent club. Failsworth Town had been run a few years back by Dave Calshaw, Graham Cook and a fella called Enda McKenna, all passionate about football but it just became too much for them through red tape and the attitude of the local council so the team sadly folded.

I did actually hear a rumour that his players once spiked poor Enda with some LSD and I think that may have been the final straw for him??

A local fella, Mark White came in as "B" team manager, and he had the chance to work with some local young rogues who I wanted to give the chance to play football. Lovable lads Roscoe, Shaun Lambert, Alan Mac, Ryan and Arran Hurst, Lee Owen, Hazey, Johnny, Fathead, Doogie and China looked more like a hoodie version of the Blazing Squad pop group when they turned out for their first training session, but I was always one for believing in young lads as no one ever showed belief in my generation at that age and myself, Mark, Alan and Pat wanted to change things.

One thing I always did and still do with all my players was talk to them like I'd expect to be spoken to. I think Mark struggled with this a bit and would constantly be at loggerheads with a few of the players as they weren't into people shouting orders at them. Mark's son Nico also joined us and was without doubt, one of the best passers of the ball I have ever seen. He had been at Blackburn as a kid and had Kenny Dalglish knocking on his door when he stopped going training. Nico told him he wasn't interested at playing at a club and just wanted to play with his mates.

The "can't be arsed" statement was one a lot of disillusioned young kids tell pro-clubs and has always baffled me?, but as the book goes on I will explain why it happens.

On the day of the final of the first Failsworth Cup, I managed to persuade local side Failsworth Dynamos to let me use their Lord Lane Pitch. I had also arranged for a celebrity football team of TV stars from Coronation St, Hollyoaks, Emmerdale etc to play against a Failsworth XI in an exhibition game as a warm up for the final. The event was well attended and I even had the players of both finalists walk out holding hands of young kids in their football kits like the Champions League Final.

A hired p.a. system also belted out the Champions League theme tune and I remember players from both the Grey Horse and Newton Heath looking at me smiling thinking I was mental. (deep down they all loved it...ha ha)

Bruno's Grey Horse F.C won both finals beating local outfits Newton Heath Railway and Moston Villa two years on the bounce, sadly due to the price of pitches I was unable to hold the tournament again as it would run at a loss. During our time doing Failsworth Town Scully and me signed some great players but also some fantastic characters and great lads.

Houghton was a huge character who came from Moston Villa and was an absolute star who I loved. The guy was as hard as nails, fit as a fiddle and had a heart of gold. Brendan Edge the manager of Moston Villa had let him go, as Houghton wanted more football. He was a great addition to us as he just made training so funny. He was without doubt the best trainer I had ever had and would give 110% every session. The best thing he had about him was his sorrow when he gave a bad pass. For example there was one game where he tried to put a through ball in for Terry Qualters, our striker. Terry made a perfect run to beat the offside but Houghton's ball went straight to the oppositions centre half. Houghton would then be saying things like "aw sorry Tez mate that was crap mate, aw terry I'm really sorry mate" while he was saying all this he would let the centre half go past him with the ball and walk up to Terry with his hand out and shake his hand. The game was totally irrelevant to him as he was more concerned about apologising for the bad pass. The line and the rest of the team would be in absolute hysterics laughing urging Houghton to forget about it quickly or the opposition would score.

Little things like that used to make getting up on a Sunday morning all worthwhile.

As I say, Houghton was a proper handy lad but nice as pie with it. I never had a problem with him until we played Failsworth Dynamos in a friendly on Mable Road. We were winning 2-0 and their manager Neil Blood had said something to Houghton, to which Houghton told him nicely to be quiet (you specky div). Neil reacted and walked on the pitch to approach him, me, Mike Taylor,

Ravo and Bucko just all looked at each other...we knew what was coming! Neil couldn't have picked the worst player on our team to have a go at, he tried giving him a slap but Houghton just chinned him and his glasses flew off in the air. Luckily everyone split it up and we finished the game with everybody calmed down. Neil and I have a laugh about it today and at least he had the balls to hold his hands up and say he was out of order. Houghton was probably the most passionate player I have ever had, and he could play a bit too. Every now and then though he would let his emotions get on top of him, and he was a bad loser. Once during a game he called our striker Mike Taylor a "fat lazy get" and said he wasn't closing down. It ended up in a few punches thrown and the referee sent Houghton off for hitting his teammate. The referee was Asian with black hair, and not at all fat... but Houghton called him a "Fat Ginger knob head?" to which we were in hysterics laughing and even the ref thought it weird and smiled.

Houghton did not have a racist bone in him so there was nothing to worry about when he got carded, and he later apologised to the referee, Mike Taylor and me. Sadly due to the nature of the sending off and the language I had to write a two page letter to the FA and I ended up getting his ban reduced from 12 months to 6 but it was the last ever match he played for me.

Other great characters that played for Failsworth Town were Hatchet and "The Check". Hatchet got his name for obvious reasons, and was like Sylvester Stallone in Escape to Victory, passionate about the game but without doubt the clumsiest football player that had ever played for me. He would actually have been a great American Football player as he would take people out for fun, and then just look at the ref with his arms out and say in his scouse accent "I never touched him ref".

The "Check" was the total opposite; he was from the Check Republic and was a pretty skilful wide player who did not speak English. His only problems were that he would get tackled (English style) and scream like a pig going to the slaughterhouse trying to get a penalty or free kick. He was constantly diving to the point where it became embarrassing and we had to educate him that it was not part of our culture in Sunday League. Other characters were Coca-Cola Pottsy, a great goalkeeper, and the local nightmare

"GAV PINDER", Gavin's lucky charm on the morning of a game was a can of Red Stripe lager. He was adamant it was something that made him play better, but it didn't wash with me and after a few weeks we parted company and he just stayed a beer buddy. Gavin and his brother Danny are huge United fans and refused to play for us when we purchased a full City kit from Bruno for the team, soz lads but once a blue always a blue!

Over the next two years we were in the Tameside Premier Sunday League and with additions of better players we were building a good football team. Three lads from Miles Platting, Shezza, Boggle and Anthony Gregory added some much needed steel to the squad and with Lee Bowles, Ratty and Kyle Wallwork we looked a decent outfit.

Kyle was Ronnie Wallworks (ex-Man United) nephew, and had been released by Man City for alleged discipline problems. He came across as being disillusioned with football and it took a while for him to get back into it. Once he did though he really loved all the lads and got on great. He started to play with a smile on his face and the team started to play some class football. There was one particular game against a team from Gorton called the Hamlet. Moston Villa needed us to beat the Gorton outfit "The Hamlet" to give them distance in the championship race, and a few of their players came to watch the game.

At half time we were down two nil and the Moston Lads were ill. I told them not to worry, as we wanted to win the game for us and not them. At half time I switched Kyle Wallwork up front and he scored the best hat trick I have ever seen. The first one was a sweet strike from about 20 yards out on the volley, which ripped the back of the net. It always sticks in my mind because the noise when the ball hit the net seemed really loud, and when you're involved in football that's got to be the best sound you can ever hear. The second was a fantastic looping header that he flicked on from a corner and went in the bottom left hand side of the net. The goalkeeper was just stood there with his hands on his head while the Moston Villa lads were going mad. The final goal was something that will stay in my head forever. Nico played a ball with the outside of his foot which seemed a bit too strong for Kyle to catch, the Hamlet defender pushed Kyle out deep into the corner, but fell on his arse. This meant the goalkeeper had to commit and he rushed out to defend his area in front of Kyle who was near the corner flag. Kyle sidestepped the goalkeeper and shot low and hard, the ball dinked against the post with venom and went in the goal. We all just stood on the line in amazement for five seconds then all went mental with the Moston boys. Considering the condition of the pitches we played on at Mellands in Gorton, it was something that will stay with me for life.

Days like these were the things that were giving me a different love for the game. As anyone involved in Amateur football will tell you, you do see some great football on a Sunday morning with some great players and great goals, it was the togetherness of the players and the staff and the laughs that was drawing me away from going to City and re-fuelling my addiction to the game. Don't get me wrong you would get some awful teams, but even then half of the lads playing in those games were doing it for the love of the game and dreaming of scoring that great goal that everyone would talk about in the pub after. That's the passion that spreads to you as a manager, and also as anyone involved in a team. It's the fact that these lads are getting up at 9.30 in the morning and playing a game after a night out on the lash. They are also not getting paid, and most are giving it 110% effort and commitment, and as a manager when you see them breaking their balls for you there is no better joy than seeing them win and achieve things they thought were impossible to achieve. This is why thousands upon thousands of amateur managers are filling water bottles and washing and ironing kits on a Saturday night for the love of it. The game would be nothing without these managers, players, league committees and understanding wives and girlfriends!

I was getting such a passion for the game I was going to local council meetings to argue that football pitches were disappearing all over North and East Manchester. We had to play our home games in Gorton and we were from Failsworth! It was the same for many local teams and it was really annoying me because over the years I had watched local councils let pitches overgrow and not maintained. They would then leave them to become eyesores for years thinking the residents would forget what they were originally for then flog them off to some building project. This is not a myth, it's a fact I was discovering while the premier league was becoming the richest league in the world, and to top it off The FA were moaning about the lack of talent coming through the system to produce world class players! As anyone involved in the amateur game will tell you, grassroots football is, and always will be the foundation of football and it is being ignored - big time.

The first local councillors meeting I went to was at Failsworth Community Centre and to tell the truth I did not know what to expect. The meeting was well attended by about 70 people and was a good mixture of all ages, from all walks of life. On the committee were the local Police Chief and a panel of local councillors mostly from the Failsworth Area. Billy Grogan, the old warhorse of local football was in attendance and also Wayne Kennedy from Failsworth Dynamos. Billy pointed me to the seat next to him, which was coincidentally next to the buffet, which was laid on for everyone. The first thing I expected him to advise to me was when to speak and who was who.

"Belting sandwiches these Simon...lovely"

He had one in each hand and was just swallowing his first.

"Sit down and just listen to some of this stuff, honestly its comical"

Billy was an old pro at local politics, and by the looks of things also an expert on the buffets at these events. Within ten minutes I understood exactly where he was coming from, councillors arguing with residents about problems that in my eyes were not even worth mentioning.

"The hanging baskets on Oldham Road have been robbed by kids".

"The pavement flags on Oldham Road are a disgrace"

"Kids are sitting outside my house smoking"

It was one after another, and to top it off when it got pretty heated the p.a system would start playing up and they all sounded like the comic Norman Collier doing his act. It became frustrating because everything I was hearing from the residents was blaming or pointing the finger at local youths. Things like this always have and always will annoy me, as I am a great believer in kids and especially the youth of today. In my eyes they are the product of us and the societies we as adults create for them. I was chomping at the bit to get up and defend them when all of a sudden the microphone was passed to a middle-aged lady who lived near our pitch on Mable Road.

"Councillors, every weekend I have to witness the bare backsides and human parts exposed of male football players on my garden wall which I find disturbing"

It rose a bit of a chuckle, especially as a lot of the women in attendance would pay for a season ticket in her front room on a Saturday and Sunday morning! This was my chance; I just jumped up without a microphone...

"I can answer that question love, the reason is because the changing rooms have been closed for 2 months and those body parts will be my players and I can only apologise."

It raised quite a laugh, but this was serious stuff to me and I was passed the microphone to get my view across. I looked at Billy who was still eating sandwiches and he just raised his eyebrows at me, as if to say "Go on" I stood up and made a bit of a speech that went along these lines,

"All I have heard tonight is problems with local youths or blame being attached to them or the local police for not doing anything. These kids are our kids, a product of our families and our neighbours. Instead of pointing the finger at the police why don't we point the fingers at ourselves, what do you as individuals do for these kids? I say this because I was once a kid who was a terror to this community as a few others in this room probably were. I am here to bring up the crisis of the lack of football pitches in this area, as well as Newton Heath and Chadderton. You may think this is not a part of our problem, but it has a huge knock on effect. If there are no facilities for kids and we are all pushing them onto the streets, what do you expect?"

I ran out of words and got speakers block, but deep down I was angry and wanted to say a million things. I was greeted to my surprise by a good round of applause and even the older folks were giving me the thumbs up. Everyone just looked at the panel awaiting a reply,

 "Simon, we have things in place that will give kids a lot more facilities in the area and we will have a chat with you later"

 As I nodded at them, I sat back down next to Billy,

"Well done, very good.........I said something similar 12 years ago"

I just looked at Billy and smiled, we knew we were banging our heads against a brick wall. For our beloved Failsworth was having a new Tesco superstore and some luxury apartments built, the cenotaph was getting revamped and there were new hanging baskets going up on Ashton Road West. We also had news that our very own sadly long departed Ben Brierley "the famous poet" was to have a statue erected in Pole Gardens with everything re-flagged and new walls built with lovely gardens!

I often wonder if Ben Brierley was a football fan, and how sad he would have been to realise the money spent on him could have gone to revamp the local youth club, or support a local kid's team that was struggling. As I write this book his statue sits in Pole Gardens of him standing proudly with a book in his hand, so he may have been a referee - Who knows???

I don't blame him as he was just put on this pedestal by history and his writing of poetry. He was probably a belting fella, and one day I promise I will read some of his poetry. His statue is currently good company to all the local skateboard kids, and I even saw a drunk one Saturday night having a full blown conversation with him for a good 10 minutes. The thing that kills me though is the guy has a plaque on the building where he was born. This is situated next to The Bridge Pub on Failsworth Pole and this historical place is now a Pizza and Kebab shop. You really could not make it up!

He has a pub named after him in Moston?? (They had a great team) and a road and school named after him in Failsworth.   I tell you what he must have been some poet, as today's modern poets like 50 cent and LL Cool J don't get anything like that and they are worldwide successes.

Poor old Ben........I swear the first trophy City win I will put a scarf round his neck. (Is that a charge sheet?)

The building of Tesco was a forgone conclusion as they are one of the biggest donators to the labour party, but baffled everyone as we had two Morrison's supermarkets within a mile of each other? As for the re-vamp of Failsworth War memorial, well that just has to be respected as people who gave their lives for this country's freedom should be the ones with statues in Pole Gardens in my eyes. The thing that annoyed me about the memorial was the price of doing it. It was a flagging job and I am sure my mate Johnny Ogden could have done it for half the price the council said it cost.

Hanging baskets??? Well I see a few of them now sitting proudly outside houses near my old school on Mather Street, and houses on Briscoe Lane in Newton Heath.

After the meeting with the council I felt an urge to do something so I wrote to every Amateur football manager in the local area to form a pitches committee. Just five managers and two councillors attended the first meeting, but we believed it was a start. We formed a Failsworth Football pitches committee, and targeted green open spaces in the area that were being left to overgrow that were council owned. We wanted to either get the council to develop them or give us leases so we could apply for grants from the Football Foundation. When I was at home I was researching constantly on the internet about pieces of land in the area, how to get grants for funding projects, how the football foundation works, the lot. The applications were all way over my head and I would spend hours studying them. I even arranged a meeting with the then Chairman of Manchester County FA Mr Jon Dutton. He was really supportive but seemed a bit dejected when I mentioned Oldham Council. He told me that the FA found them to be the hardest council to work with, and they had not had a lot of luck with them in the past, but he would help me in anyway he could.

He told me our pitches committee's first task was to get a 25 year lease for the land and then the FA would step in and help us.

As I write this now four years later we still do not have a lease, after promises and promises. This annoys me as all the council have to do is give a lease to a "Charter Standard" organisation which we are, and then other funding would develop the land for the council's community and they would get the land with a facility on it back in 25 years. SIMPLE you would think - I'm afraid not.

Fifteen years ago (1996) Failsworth had over eight football pitches for senior teams and two for juniors. Now it has just two senior and two junior pitches that are open on hire to teams in the area. Newton Heath, which comes under Manchester Council, has just one senior pitch and NO kid's pitches with changing rooms.

Yes!! Newton Heath the birthplace of the FA's pride and joy MANCHESTER UNITED, the richest club in the world (second richest now).

To top it off my very own Manchester City's new stadium is called Sports City. My club lease the stadium fromathe council, it is called "THE CITY OF MANCHESTER STADIUM" in "SPORTS CITY" It is situated next to Miles Platting, Beswick and Ancoats, which are in a worst predicament than us for football pitches. City's reserves play in the athletics stadium, which is only used in the week for games. So being Sports City owned by Manchester Council, leased by MCFC (who got a lease quicker than us) you would think the people of Manchester would be able to play a few Sunday League finals on City's ground, and be able to hire the reserves pitch for Saturday and Sunday football teams in the local area?? Not a chance. I spent two hours one day on the phone asking Manchester Council if I could hire the Athletic/reserve pitch for a Sunday team. I was given a circle of phone numbers and not one person would give me an answer or the reason why these "public" facilities were not available to the community. They just passed the buck and knocked me all over the show. This is a disgrace in my eyes considering the amount of football talent in those areas being totally neglected. Why should kids in Newton Heath, Ancoats, Miles Platting, Collyhurst, Beswick have to travel to other places and areas to play football for other areas teams. Well you decide? Apartments? Open spaces? Property Development? Price of Land? Weird???

The fight goes on, and I will tell you now, we will never win the world cup till it is sorted out, as this problem is NATIONWIDE in all cities in the UK.

Football can be used as a fantastic tool but in today's society people involved in authority purely for personal reasons surround us. Since I have been writing this book the Manchester Evening news has revealed a sorry state of affairs concerning the proposed building of a new Stadium on land on Broadway in Failsworth for Oldham Athletic.

This was land that was earmarked by the council and Failsworth Dynamos to be developed into football pitches for local grassroots football. Again even though I do not know the full plans, this is another slap in the face for football in the area where I live. Failsworth in the past 20 years has lost eight football pitches for grassroots teams to land development projects.

Sadly because this happens over time and evolves, nobody notices and nobody protests as they become blind to it. Councillors move on and the local people lose out to losing greens spaces and facilities. I read stories of this happening all over the country with clubs and football leagues folding with their cries unheard.

The FA to be fair are doing a good job working with certain councils, but sadly my experience with Oldham Council is nothing positive at all. They have constantly told me and others lie after lie and never come up with the goods when it comes to football in the Borough.

Football breaks down barriers of racial divide, social divide and all sorts of diversity issues yet sadly I see no signs of it being used in my area to its full potential. Oldham has suffered more than other areas with these issues in the past and it has led to racial tensions in the area. Yet sadly these tensions continue to boil while the council looks at selling off its green spaces behind a cloak and dagger image and ignoring the great tool of football that can solve these problems.

Still like many others volunteers up and down the country, I will continue to shout for kids and future generations who love the game and believe it can heal so many wounds and build so many bridges to improve our society. The evidence is staring us and the governing bodies straight in the face! I believe every season the professional bodies of football should hold a ROOTS week. It's an idea I believe would have a great impact on the game and bring the football family closer together.

The idea would be that every professional football player in the world donates a week's wage to a local amateur football team in the community where that particular player was born or raised. The club would host the player for a full day at a function showing their appreciation to this player on his end of season time. As you can imagine this would kick start so much activity at grassroots level and be a huge income for grassroots football globally.

It would be just one weeks wage to sacrifice for the player, but I am sure he would get it back in the work he would see it was being used for.

For example:-

Paul Scholes   -   £60k donated to clubs in Oldham

Stephen Gerrard   -   £130k donated to clubs in Liverpool

John Terry   -   £130k donated to clubs in London.

Robiniho   -   £150k donated to clubs in Sao Paulo

The government could even do their bit by making this tax-free so the full wage went to the community clubs. Can you imagine the positive impact that this would have on the game?? Immense!

This would be so simple to organise and I am sure would make fantastic TV for Sky Sports by showing where the money goes to and the impact it has had on the communities and clubs. Football fans are always complaining about how much money stars are on, and I believe it would soften the blow if they saw them giving a little back.

I have been to countless FA meetings on how to improve the game in the local communities and in my eyes it is so simple. Build a full 4-G synthetic football pitch in every community and town in Great Britain. I have seen first hand how they can improve football and the standard that is played.

Anyone involved in the game at grassroots level will tell you the problem in our country is the cost of maintaining grass pitches. Today's synthetic pitches are better than grass as the ball moves quicker and is more precise when passed around the pitch. They are also easier and more cost effective to maintain and can be played on 365 days a year.

This means better football and wider participation by more football teams at all levels. There is nothing worse in the game than seeing a 10 year old make a great pass only for the ball to get stuck in mud and see the opposing team score from it. You cannot tell a kid to pass the ball on a mud bath that has rut's of mud all over the pitch, so coaches nature tell their players to hoof it which contradicts everything they teach in training.

Many of us involved in amateur football dream one day that this becomes reality and the players, FA and most importantly councils see how much of an impact this could have on society in general.

CHAPTER 5

"OUR CLUB"

Club: an organisation made up of members who sustain it and make decisions and support it in all things by discussion and voting?

Even though I was doing Sunday Football I was still a mad City fan. We were moving into a new stadium, Kevin Keegan had took us into the premiership and things were looking up, I still attended the match when I could but tried to steer clear of trouble.

Like all city fans I was gutted to leave Maine Road as it had so many great memories, the pubs, pie shops, kebab shops, the ticket touts, Mikey Williams (R.I.P.), The Kippax, the list is endless. A move to the old Commonwealth stadium was too good to turn down, and it would be "a great move for the club" the fans we were told. The first worrying sign for everyone was when the owners changed the Manchester City badge from the round one to the one we know now with the eagle and three stars??? It was done in my eyes without the permission of the fans and purely for marketing purposes. It still hurts me today and it was something I look back on and think we, as fans should never have allowed.

As football fans we do not realise the power and influence we should have, and could have if we all got our heads together. We as fans pay for these (OUR) clubs to exist yet we play second fiddle to the owners when they make decisions between themselves purely to make money and fleece us.

It's a bit like shopping in Morrisons, all of a sudden they get in all foreign food and put the prices go up ten fold and change the location of their superstore and change the brand. You would just stop going and change to Tesco or Sainsburys. The thing is football owners and the authorities have got us by the balls, as they know we love the clubs and won't change because we can't. So they evolve change slowly so we don't notice, i.e. prices, merchandise, rules, standing etc etc.

If you put a frog in a cold pan of water and slowly heat it up it will sit there till it boils to death unaware of the danger.

If you throw a frog in hot water it will straight away try and escape as it can sense the danger to its life and is quickly aware of it.

We as human beings behave exactly the same it is how "ALL" big corporate businesses plan strategies throughout the world. It's how governments including our own councils treat us as a population. It's how they initiate things such as "Police States" i.e. CCTV, fingerprints, I.D cards, Passports, Section 60, Freedom of Rights, they do it gradually. The Poll Tax (riots) were renamed as the council tax (no riots)?

THEY DO IT GRADUALLY! Are you getting the message?

In my eyes football clubs and the relevant governing bodies are using exactly the same tactic. My club were no different!

When you ask me about Manchester City the first thing that comes in my head is the round badge, then the sky blue kit with a red and black away kit, Colin Bell, Maine Road, standing on the Kippax, every match being affordable, Then it was a fans club supporting it's supporters (all of them)!

Is this the same club we supported, that still exists today? I ask myself sometimes, this was something I was watching happen and I was waiting for someone, or some bodies to say something, Supporters clubs, ex-players, Official Supporters Clubs, the media? Who was I - what could I do? Nothing??

The first few games at the new stadium most city fans were starting to notice new things and new rules that weren't in place at Maine Road. There was no warning it just happened and no one was saying or doing a thing about it. We would watch as Stewards would come in as snatch squads and grab young and old fans for singing and standing. I was hearing testimonies of blues getting threatened and told off other blues to sit down in their seats and shut up singing. Fans were getting season tickets confiscated for pathetic things like smoking, swearing and yes.... SINGING. I was fuming, it was becoming like a cinema rather than a football stadium. Come in and buy some over priced food, sit down, be quiet and watch the match. Oh... and buy a membership card for £10 so you can "Purchase a ticket" no card no ticket. The atmosphere was shocking, there was no co-ordination, the whole thing was a mess. It was like mixing gunpowder (singers) with flour (normal fans) and expecting a spark to ignite it. It just was not going to happen, as none of the stands had any identity and fans from the old Kippax, Maine Stand, Platt Lane and North Stand were all mixed in. The club had given it no thought about the effect this would have, it was causing murders and fighting between blues almost every week. It was killing me and other blues, but no one was doing anything. The Manchester Evening news got a few letters of complaint but nothing, no supporters clubs... not a sausage (bar Don Price and the Prestwich and Whitefield mob).

It got to the point where I felt I had to try to do something as this was the club I loved and no way could I just sit there and watch this happen. Loyal fans for years being told how they were to support "OUR" club after years of following them, and getting physically abused in the process.

There was one crazy idea a few fans had of creating a vigilante group and asking all the "guvnors" to protect the fans from the stewards by giving them back what they gave out. A bit like the Ultra's, but then I think everyone woke up and realised they would get about ten years for conspiracy!

I was, and still am a staunch supporter of standing at matches, and like many other fans I wasn't happy when we went to all seated stadiums because of the Tailor Report after the Hillsboro disaster. The reasons lives were lost were because of poor policing, poor stewarding and bad organisation. Instead standing got the blame, which was a fantastic get out clause for all involved. The Taylor report created the "Football Licensing Authority" whose roll it is to check stadiums have the correct resources for spectators. It wasn't long ago named as one of the top ten "KWANGO'S" (*basically a blag authority that does nothing*) in the United Kingdom.

Due to my anger on these issues I started to do research on the Internet and go on many City websites. I also started writing articles in City fanzines such as "King Of The Kippax" and "City Till I Cry". I wanted to speak out about my anger and dismay of the way our club and game was going. If I could see it surely everyone else could, something needed to be done. I started to meet great City fans like Phil Gatenby (Safestanding), Dave Wallace (King Of The Kippax), Tom Ritchie (City Till I Cry) and last but not least Don Price of Prestwich and Whitefield Supporters Club. These were blues who had been fighting for the fans for years over topical stuff like the "Swales Out" campaign and I felt they understood me. Phil Gatenby was, and still is the most passionate football fan I have ever met. Phil had been fighting to bring safe standing back to the game for years but the media and the authorities were just ignoring people like him. He helped me create a group called "The Atmosphere Action Group". This was just a group of fans that were unhappy with the atmosphere and new policies installed at our new stadium.

We held our first meeting at The Railway pub in Hollinwood just outside Failsworth. The Railway is a big City fans pub and we had arranged for Peter Fletcher (Stadium Safety Officer) and Sara Billington (Head of Operations) to attend the meeting to represent the club. After advertising in the M.E.N. and on City websites the meeting was poorly attended by about 20 blues. Most had been ejected from the ground and had their season tickets confiscated for standing constantly and complaints from other fans. The meeting went ok but a few fans were really angry and a fair bit of shouting went on so we had to end it. In the group of City fans was, believe it or not, one of the clubs directors David Makin! He just looked like a normal lad to me, he put over some really good points and it seemed weird that someone who part owned the club was putting questions to his employees. In the end I think Peter And Sara clocked him and were really baffled by it all. I was later told that Mr Makin was a passionate North Stand Blue when we were at Maine Road and he was unhappy at how the fans were being treated and wanted to show his support. Fair play to the fella!

During this time I also became involved with safestanding.co.uk. This was a pro-active organisation that was doing things how I wanted to do things....protest. After a lot of dialogue with their committee who were all West Ham fans we decided to organise a few protests at different games. We printed over 8000 yellow cards that were to be held up just before kick-off, in protest over the fact that some fans wanted the right to stand. Safe standing was available to fans in Holland and Germany so why not here??

Myself and a lad called Ste O'Mara were interviewed by Sky Sports before a home match against United to get our message nationwide. The protest went well but we couldn't hand out all the cards in time as we did not have enough distributors. Then we (The Atmosphere Action Group) got slated off the press as everyone made paper planes with the cards and through them onto the pitch.

Other protests in London at West Ham and Spurs games went really well and the organisation still fights today to bring safe standing back. Currently though as we speak fans are still being ejected in grounds all over the country for trying to support their team in the only way they know how...standing and singing. It made me laugh at one fans meeting I attended a few years back when one person who I won't name asked, "Why can't fans sit down and sing - I just don't see the problem?" You just could not make it up!

At a typical meeting with the MCFC fans committee the fans discuss topics to bring up with the clubs chairman and directors. Then four people are asked to volunteer to re-attend the ground for the meeting to put their questions forward. The first time I volunteered I attended with my friend Tom Ritchie the editor of the fanzine "City Till I Cry", Phil Gatenby from the Football

Fans Federation and two other fans who I cannot remember. I do remember being nervous as hell waiting in the lobby of the new stadium on a Tuesday afternoon. Here I was, a known casual (Guvnor) at the match about to represent the fans of the club I loved so dearly. Me, Simon Cooper of Failsworth, this couldn't be right I was saying to myself.

Other members of the delegation turned up and we were shown into the clubs boardroom and offered light refreshments while we waited for the hierarchy of the club I had followed as a child. The room looked over the pitch and I was constantly thinking to myself what the hell was I doing here. I was nervous but I was passionate about the way I felt the club were mistreating its' fans and I wanted to get those points across to the Chairman and his directors, I just couldn't sit there week after week and watch while nothing was done. The door opened and in walked Sara Billington who was "Head Of Operations", Alistair McIntosh "Chief Executive" and the Chairman John Wardle. We were introduced and we sat down about five foot from each other, the main delegate for the fans went through the topics that were raised and started from the top.

Some of the topics I felt were embarrassing, such as the quality of snack foods, the time it took to get a pint at half time, smoking in the aisles, traffic problems getting home from the match etc etc. I was here for just two things, standing and the mistreatment of my fellow supporters. As I waited I noticed that the Chairman and his associates were just as bored as me with the topics I've just mentioned and to be honest I don't blame them. Things like that should stay in hand written letters in my mind, and I was sure they would quietly agree.

I always remember looking at John Wardle and the guy looked absolutely shattered. I was thinking to myself this guys got players contracts to sort out, the press, finances and loads of other things and I'm sat here with a fans delegation with some of them asking him why the half time tea, coffee and snack bar service is so poor! I was embarrassed at times for him, the committee, and everyone in attendance.

I once went to the bar in the ground at half time during a match and asked for a pint of lager and a packet of salt and vinegar crisps. The oriental guy came back with a pint and gave me my change, to which I said "Hey mate where's my Salt and Vinegar crisps?" He just looked at me strange and replied….. "We no do RIBS!" The full queue just pissed themselves laughing. I mean what chance have you got of having a good service if your employee's cannot speak or understand English. The poor blokes got no chance has he?

My turn eventually came to get my points over and to be honest the nerves had gone as I was that passionate about what I wanted to say. "Mr Chairman, I am really worried about the way the club is treating it's supporters. There are new rules installed in this stadium that are stopping passionate fans from being able to support their team as they did at Maine Road. These new rules we believe, were never announced to the fans and in the long run will push fans away and stop them from attending the match. Also I find it disgusting that fans are now asked to pay for a membership card just to be able to purchase a ticket. I believe this is just a marketing scheme to bleed the fans of yet more money. I speak to blues at work, in the pub and in the Manchester area and they are all becoming very disillusioned with how this club is treating it's loyal fans. Whatever happened to the club that "Supports it's Supporters", why all of a sudden are stewards becoming like Nazi snatch squads"

It definitely woke him up, and to be quite truthful he did not seem that knowledgeable about it and looked a bit shocked. I told them if these things did not change soon within 18 months attendances would be below 40,000. How did I know? Because I saw the hardcore City fans day in day out and I lived in Manchester.

They explained to me that the Football Licensing Authority and Manchester City Council were putting severe pressure on them and would close the ground if they did not comply or implement these rules. Phil Gatenby asked why did they not announce these rules with the fans before the club moved stadiums, and why would they not stand up for these fans and fight the council and the Football Licensing Authority, at the end of the day surely they had to represent all fans feelings?

I won't quote what was replied but they made it quite clear that they were scared to death of the council and the Football Licensing Authority, and their hands were tied. This angered us all and I told them passionately they would lose thousands of fans very soon and they were going to end up with a lot of upset fans and low gates. Their reply was that the club could not foresee this as they had an 8000 season ticket waiting list and there were well-behaved fans waiting to replace badly behaved fans. Myself, Tom and Phil all just looked at each other in amazement, I knew from that day what our club was about. Come to your own conclusion but it really knocked me for six, these people just did not see what we could see clear as day. This was not the Manchester City that I had grown up to love as my club, what were these people doing?

Over the next twelve months more and more fans were banned, season tickets revoked and some received criminal records. This had not happened at Maine Road and it was knocking me sick, and I mean physically sick. The membership card price went up and guess what gates dropped dramatically.

In our first season at the new stadium under Kevin Keegan we were sold out virtually every week, the following season I saw the signs early on, the Thomas Cook Trophy's attendance was only about 25,000 ok, it's only a friendly but I knew how City fans were taking it. What the club didn't realise was that these fans who they were banning were friends of other blues and the word was spreading like wild fire…. "You can't go to the game anymore and enjoy yourself…its shite, the atmospheres shit as well, you're not sat next to anyone who you know….I've had enough, I'm not paying money to be treated like an animal"

The thing is with City fans you have to understand our mentality, we have been without a trophy for over 30 years and people wonder why we still get huge gates and huge away followings in that time, the fact of the matter is City fans go to the match for the "crack" the day out, to meet friends, get away from home life for a few hours, have a laugh and see some football.

Example…

"Oh we never win at home and we never win away

we lost last week and we lost today

we don't give a f**k coz were all p**sed up

MCFC OK."

We've been doing it for years, and now you're trying to take that away from us! We have had to have that mentality because we've won nothing for 30 years. So all of a sudden some clever dick comes along and tries taking our bread and butter away! You can see where I'm coming from now... I know you can. I don't speak for all blues but a damn majority of the diehards!

It's probably the same for a lot of fans all over the country, and I'm led to believe from a lot of United fans its even worse at O.T, the sad thing for United is the waiting list for them is never ending, so there will be always someone, somewhere who will gladly snap up a season ticket no matter what. I know so many Mancunian reds that have stopped attending for exactly the same reasons. Anyway the attendances dropped and dropped and within 18 months our prediction had born fruit. We were correct and we were hitting as low as 38,000 for some matches. So with the 8000 season ticket waiting list gone we had lost over 16,000 fans in 18 months. You can say they were "Johnny Come Lately's" but I believe they were real fans, and a lot of passionate fans. Strange thing was after the gates dropped the stewards all of a sudden relaxed a little bit and were starting to be nice to the fans. Weird hey???

Things like this were pushing so many City fans away from watching, me included. People like Phil Gatenby and my mate Don Price, a fantastic bloke and a great blue who was the foundation of the Prestwich and Whitefield branch of City supporters. If he was becoming disillusioned, in my eyes the club were messing up big time. These sorts of fans the club could not afford to lose, I was really ticked off as the club were not listening, it wasn't just our club it was the whole of the Premier League's Football clubs, and they were treating their fans like dirt.

It was about this time that some Manchester United fans formed their own breakaway club and I watched with interest and things started going on in my head. Life at City was becoming unbearable

Simon Cooper

for many blues as the match day atmosphere was being robbed in broad daylight every week and it was getting worse and worse.

CHAPTER 6

"FANS FOOTBALL CLUB"

In 2004, fans all over the country were becoming really upset with the way football was going. No more so than at our neighbours Manchester United. A business family from America were worrying sections of their fans about the possible takeover of the club. Anyway you know the rest and after many a harsh word FC United, the fans club was formed by Andy Walsh and other Manchester United fans. Many City fans laughed at this and took the piss out of United as the club seemed in turmoil, and at the time it was quite funny watching all the commotion on sky sports.

United fans were falling out with each other and it was comical as well as a dream for many City fans to see the club's fans divided on the issue. I was looking a little deeper though and I understood where they were coming from, I could see through all the red mist that many City fans found hilarious.

Here were loads of passionate Manchester United fans ready to walk away from a club they had loved and sacrificed so much for, and in my eyes it was something to be respected, but as a football fan you had to go deep within yourself to understand it.

Manchester United for the first time in it's history that was going to be owned by outsiders who had no feelings about the club and just saw it as a business deal. They had no previous affiliation to the club and the fans were worried, they predicted heavy debt, high admission prices and that the club would cut off many working class fans by pricing them out of "Gold Trafford."

What those fans did was one of the bravest things, I believe has ever happened in football. They received abuse from fellow fans and even Alex Ferguson was having slight digs at them in the press and in the media. This was the biggest supported football club in the world and it was having a revolution, it was an amazing thing to watch. It was a bunch of fans standing up for the history of this once working class club by saying, "Hey this is Manchester United, new owners come and go but the fans are here forever. Have you forgot about us who supported you in the dark days??"

I felt exactly the same about my club Manchester City, they were treating the fans like crap, hiking up prices, bringing in membership cards, and had in my eyes stopped supporting its supporters. They were also pushing people to the brink of divorce from the club they had loved all their lives. The fact of the matter was this was happening, and still is up and down the country at all the major clubs.

At City in the first season at Coms, the sold out signs were up and the club had the power to pick and choose its fans. I really think the board thought Manchester City could become a Manchester United and they were using the reds as a blueprint of how to make money. The thing is City's hierarchy obviously didn't have an understanding of their fans and did not take these two points on board.

Manchester United have a huge fan base due to their success under Ferguson and the history of the Munich air disaster. A fan that stops going can always be replaced by a fan with more money, and they know replacing them will not be a problem.

Manchester City fans are not as vast in numbers, and once you crap on them they don't forget it. The club do not have the resources and mentality of fans to work the same way. At this time though the club in my opinion were of the thought "Hey we have an 8000 season ticket waiting list here, we can do the same"

So as the previous chapter states, gates went down and if you add the 8000 fans on the waiting list we lost 16,000 fans in 18 months. This is an amazing statistic and one I cannot still to this day realise how no one picked up on. I have always said if City had a capacity of 70,000 fans, put the prices down and treated the fans how they wanted treating, they would fill it every game. Many of you might laugh, but I am deadly serious and history backs my theory up. We still hold the highest gate in a domestic home game, 84,000 plus - where the hell did all those fans go? Surely they had kids and grandkids??

I'm telling you now, if you put admission prices to £10 for adults and £5 for kids you could get 70,000 blues in a ground for most games. To prove this theory write down on a piece of paper how many blues you know go week in week out. Then write down how many blues you know who don't go because they cannot afford to take their families. My first list of blues who go week in week out is 15. My second list of blues who don't go week in week out (most watch it on TV in the pub) is 79 plus their kids!!!

I am sure many of you come up with similar statistics, and you know deep down those people would attend if they could afford to take their family's week in week out. I swear if I ever win the lottery I will buy that club and install those admission prices and extend the capacity to prove the point. The marketing at City and United is purely for financial reasons and both clubs are blind to the fact that they have the capability of attracting so many more fans by just the simple introduction of cheap admission. If we did lower the prices would it cripple the club? How the hell could it, they would sell more merchandise, hamburgers, drinks etc and they now receive millions more on television rights so the gate money is second fiddle to TV income.

If they designated different stands for different fans they would create a better atmosphere and the match would become more memorable. The current stands are after 5 years just now gaining an identity for singing. Block 111 Blue Square boys, and the South stand singing sections are now boosting the stadiums atmosphere every week and becoming better and better. One night I received a phone call from someone who is a wealthy businessman and a huge blue who I will not name. He asked me what I thought of the

FC United thing and did I agree with it? We had a long chat and after the call I was adamant this was the way forward for "some" of us as City fans to go. To break away and reform our own club with the traditions and treatment of fans we believed, as fans were right for us. Manchester City and Manchester United in this day and age only have three connections to Manchester:-

The first one is their name... Manchester

The second one is they play in Manchester...

The third one is most of their fans come from Manchester.

Both clubs have foreign owners who want to make them globally supported, make them richer and bigger assets so they can sell them on and make a few quid. Both clubs badges have changed, supporters clubs are dying all over the place and many working class fans are being pushed away by high prices.

I and others spoke to a good few blues about the idea, and many were 100% in agreement but would not help getting involved. We went on loads of City websites such as bluemoon-mcfc, cool as duck, mancityfans.net and also looked at how FC United were working. We set up an e-mail address for supporters to give me their feedback and I was shocked at how upset some fans were with the club after brutal treatment. I received over 600 e-mails of support from blues who said they were miffed off with how the game and the match day experience was becoming. Some of them were really moving and a few put lumps in my throat, they were that serious.

Here were City fans that had been passionately following City home and away for years and they had come to the end of the line. The club was changing, the game was changing, fans wanted out. These were not traitors, these were blues who just simply couldn't afford to go anymore or handle how their so called club was treating them.

Within days we arranged a meeting for all interested supporters in forming a rebel club to attend a meeting in Mary Dee's near the stadium. Using the City internet sites we chose 15 people to attend with all different skills that hopefully could form a committee. The meeting was well attended and we decided to call the venture FFC City. It stood for Fans Football Club City, and the group seemed really positive and determined. I remember walking away from that meeting thinking this was going to be one hell of a commitment and we would receive pure abuse for it and people would drop out.

When we were researching the idea, we were amazed to find that Manchester City already had a fans football club that had already been created by fans nearly 50 years ago. The name of that club was Maine Road FC, it was perfect! Myself and 3 other members of the committee made contact with the Maine Road club and we met with a few of their directors at their Brantingham Road home in Chorlton. It was a stones throw from City's old ground and we were all excited at the prospect of offering blues a cheaper alternative of watching a local blue club.

On arrival Mr Barber and a few of his colleagues met us, and they seemed rightly so, a bit apprehensive. They informed us they had seen all this before but they were very interested in the prospect of new fans, especially City fans.

Sadly due to threats to some of the members of the committee, the venture became weaker and weaker. Many supporters ridiculed the idea and said we were not in the same boat as United fans as our club was owned by City fans and we were just a bunch of idiots. It was water off a ducks back to me, but sadly some of the other members took it to heart and disappeared which left only a handful of us, and it became just too much work. We still received e-mails from hundreds of players and coaches from all over the country who wanted in and looking back it would have been more than possible to achieve building that club with the right people involved. I attended Maine Road matches several times and I can honestly say it is a great club and I thoroughly enjoyed every match. They play in blue, have a badge like the old City badge which I love and all the owners are passionate City fans. Good old Derek Barber once played for City and is a football mad guy who makes sure that all their teams play football how it should be. If you ever get the chance and have an empty Saturday afternoon, just have a look at their website for fixtures. Pies,

Bovril and standing at the game, it's a great feeling and takes you back to what football is really about. Lads playing for the love and passion of the game, volunteers devoting and sacrificing their lives to commit to keeping the club alive. The club have produced many players over the years who have moved on to play at the highest level, non-more so then one of my best friends Colin Little who went on to play for Crewe Alexandra for many years. Colin is a passionate blue and even scored against City when he played at Maine Road and I know still keeps an eye out for the clubs results.

FC United, at this time were well organised and were being well supported all over the northwest counties. My first experience of actually seeing them was by accident at Curzon Ashton's new ground. I was attending a Tameside Sunday League inter-league fixture on the Astroturf pitch the same night they had a fixture at the stadium. I was shocked at how the fans treated the game, it was like an FA cup final and the ground was rammed with an electric atmosphere. All of my mates watched from over the fence with a few of the inter-league players. The songs were constant and really funny with scarves swinging round throughout every verse. I remember the Stretford end in Uniteds 'Dave Sexton' era and it was the closest thing I have ever seen to it. To be honest as a City fan and a football fan I was jealous, as it looked a fantastic crowd and was like something you see abroad, but on a smaller scale. This was something that was missing in today's Premier League and these United fans had grasped it and brought it back to the place of its birth......... grassroots football. It made me realise that the game I once sacrificed so much for to go and watch had changed, and the closest replacement I could find for it was amateur football.

Being disillusioned with City and the premier league money machine, I was now totally devoted to my Sunday League team. I was more than happy to replace paying £100 for an away day watching City with managing my team Failsworth Town on Mellands in Gorton on a weekend.

We were doing pretty well and as the season came to an end I was looking at turning us into a Saturday team. This after research was basically impossible through lack of decent facilities in the local area and the cost of running the team due to league fees and other stuff. At the end of the season though I received a surprise phone call that was one, being a kid I could never have even dreamed of.

CHAPTER 7

"THE FOOTBALL PYRAMID"

As I've said earlier on, and I'd like to clarify, I never have been, nor am I, a big time hard man football hooligan who has changed his ways and is now trying to play Mr nice guy. I have also never been a great football player, in fact I was never an average football player and some people would say manager either, I just love the game and have always given everything 100% effort in anything I do.

Sometimes in life you can be totally oblivious to the fact that people are watching you and that you're work is getting noticed. I haven't ever done things in my life to get noticed or get plaudits, I have done them purely because it's something I enjoy and gain self-achievement from. I have always been advised I am not good enough or have not got the right pedigree to do certain things in my life, especially amateur football.

That's one of the main things I love about football, it gives the underdog the chance to come out a winner. I remember certain football players, many lads I have grown up with telling me I could never be a good manager. It just spurred me on to prove them wrong by giving me an extra boost to go the extra mile. When I did things like the Failsworth Cup tournament I knew people did not believe that I could pull it off. The biggest supporter I have ever had is myself, and that is through my mum giving me that instinct. I remember her working all the hours god sent to put our Louis and me in the best clothes she could afford and a clean house with a roof over our heads. We would get abuse at school for our family's religion, which would end up in me having fight after fight and being bullied by older lads. This is not a sob story it's just something I wanted to mention as it made me tougher in later life and taught me not to listen to anyone except the people who mattered... your family.

My mum always instilled into us that it did not matter what everyone else said or talked about, what mattered was what we knew in our hearts was right. She taught us always to believe in our own ability and listen to nobody except people who had achieved the goals we were striving for. That was something I had always set in stone in my head and why I had always respected local football managers like Phil "Bruno" Brown, Johnny Ham and Terry Pickup. These guys had been doing football for years and I always listened to them and never disputed anything they shared with me. If anyone else talked to me about football that had not been there and done it, then it went in one ear and out the other. It taught me a lot and it was the foundation of how I became an amateur football manager.

One evening during July 2007, I received a phone call from Dave Moxon, the secretary of a local Saturday football club called Avro F.C, at first I thought he was going to ask me for a friendly game but to my amazement he was offering me the opportunity to be first team manager. After arranging to meet him in my local pub for a chat I put the phone down and just thought to myself this is a wind up!

No matter where you live in this country there will be a big, local amateur football team that everyone aspires to play for. In Failsworth it was always Avro Football Club who were the old workers team from British Aerospace. The club is based on Broadway at the junction of Oldham Road and has a history going back to before the war.

When I was at school a lot of my schoolmates would talk about it in very high esteem. It was the creme-da-la-creme of local football and if you played for them you were basically the dogs bollocks. The pitches are second to only the top tier of English football, and the clubhouse is like something you would see at a premier league club. The quality is that good, Oldham Athletic hire the club for its facilities and pitches, as well as doing their pre-season training on there. Over the years many good ex-players such as Len Cantello (WBA), Tommy Booth (MCFC) and most recently Louis Chalmers (Aldershot) have gone on to forge a career in the game. It has always been and still is seen as a possible stepping-stone into full time football. As I thought of these things I just sat back in my chair and looked at the ceiling, me Simon Cooper... Failsworth "B" team substitute manager of Avro football club... you're having a laugh?" I just smiled and thought to myself "You don't win the lottery if you don't buy a ticket"

I had been doing Sunday League for 5 years and to tell the truth the state of the pitches and attitudes of some players and opposing teams was getting to me. Like a lot of managers I was sick of paying out of my own pocket for fines and equipment and sick of dragging players out of bed. (I had a couple of particular players who could be in anyone of 6 different girls beds on a Sunday morning, and I was sick of chasing players who I know were having sex while talking to me on the phone of a morning!)

Avro was in my eyes the "Real Madrid" of local amateur football and I would be mad to turn it down. They had just been relegated from the Manchester Amateur Premier League and from what information I could gather were in a mess on and off the pitch.

I met Dave Moxon the secretary, the club captain Dave Thornton and Steve Gavin who was one of the senior players in the Windmill pub for an interview and a chat. To tell the truth I was a bit overawed and couldn't understand why I had been chosen as there were so many more experienced people in the area. I wasn't going to give them any ideas so I just kept quiet and let them talk. After an hour of chatting and a few handshakes I became the manager of Avro Football Club, and to say I was proud would be an understatement.... I was ecstatic!

When I got home I explained to my wife, Mandy the relevance of the job. To me it was like moving from a Vauxhall Conference club to a Premier League club that had been relegated. She just looked at me and smiled, she knew it would totally cut me off from watching City and getting in at daft o'clock, and she could now have her dream family Sunday days.

For me to be offered the job I knew the club would be in a mess, but on my first meeting with Dave Moxon I was astounded to see the lack of equipment and kit the club actually had. We needed kits, balls, cones, bibs, bottles kitbags the lot, it made me realise the first team structure was on its arse. After a long chat with Dave we shared some fundraising ideas and we used a great organisation called Sponsorbank to help us get some grants for the club (not as easy as you think)

(Things like this annoy me about football, the pyramid of football is starving at the bottom while the top is totally creaming it. Without the bottom of the pyramid the premier league would not exist but it seems to forget about it's foundations too easily. If every premier league player in Manchester sacrificed and donated one weeks wage a year, the whole area could sustain healthy football clubs for many years. It's that simple!)

A lot of people warned me that that I would not last as the club was very clicky. The word "politics" was always attached to the club, which I never fully understood at first but later on in the year it did reveal itself.

After the first training session I realised that I had to bring in new players and it dawned on me then how much of a huge job I had in front of me. The main problem was "respect" and I quickly realised that the existing players looked at me for what I was, "a Sunday league manager who had never played the game at any decent level" After having a long think about it I knew it would do me a favour as these players would be the first out of the door and I could bring lads I knew would fight tooth and nail for me. To start though I wanted to give everyone a chance so I mixed the reserves with the old first team players and told all of them they had a clean slate. After talking to a few of the squad on their own I realised a lot of them believed if your face did not fit then you had no chance of getting in the first team. This became more and more convincing when I used to go in the clubhouse and see the two sets of lads from the same club sat in different rooms. It annoyed me because I knew we had to have a squad mentality if we were to be successful. I arranged a couple of friendly games with FC United reserves and also Blackley FC out of the Premier League. I asked a good friend of mine called Bobby Jones to do the pre-season training as he was a quality coach and I knew he could take them to the level we needed to be at.

I never classed myself as a great coach and I always stressed that to the players, but once Bobby did a few sessions I think they wanted me doing them again. Bobby is a schoolteacher and was a quality football player who had played for a host of semi-professional clubs. The way he applies his sessions on the players was something that I have soaked up in my head over the years. He simplifies everything and speaks with a voice of authority but on the other side of the coin it comes across as respectful to the players. He just describes everything so basic, and makes tactics work like a dream. During pre-season I was constantly on the phone trying to get more players I knew to sign on, I was surprised that a lot of them were so negative about the club, and again the word "politics" rose it's ugly head. These were players I had known for years and I thought would thrive at the challenge.

"Nothing against you mate, but I hate the place" "It's too clicky mate, it's not for me" I was flabbergasted at some of the responses but even so I managed to get a few players in that I knew could make a difference. Over the next ten weeks Michael McLaughlin (Boggle), Dale Cook, Ryan Shaunessy, Chris Faulkner, Mike Taylor, Tony Nightingale, Martin Dale, 'Nico' White, and Kyle Wallwork, to name just a few would sign up. A few eyebrows were raised in the clubhouse and word started spreading that I had brought some "unsavoury characters to the club". I wasn't worried though because I brought lads in who I knew could apply the job I wanted them to do on the pitch, what they did off it was nobody's business, including the Lancaster Club's. I had learnt some people needed to be given a second chance in life and I was not going to deprive any player of that chance. All I asked them to do was behave on the pitch and respect the staff, their fellow players and me.

The first training sessions were pretty nervous, and to tell the truth I did not know what sort of response I was going to get, yes I knew a few of the players but these lads had low morale and it was obvious that their attitude could make things really easy or very difficult. The captain was a belting lad called Dave Thornton, but due to injury he had missed a few training sessions so I decided to ruffle a few feathers by swapping the armband about. Pre-season training went well due to the help of my mate Bobby Jones, his communication skills and application are second to none, he makes sessions hard but enjoyable and this had a major impact on the lads.

I organised a pre-season friendly with FC United reserves which we drew 2-2 and we also played Blackley FC which was also 2-2. We had played well in both games but I was worried about the size of the squad and the state of the reserve team. I sat down with all the players and told them that it was a concern to me and that the first team and the reserve team would be no longer - we were to become a squad. In my eyes the reserves had to have players good enough to be pushing the first team. I would go in the club bar and see so called first team players sat in one corner and the so-called reserves in another corner. It used to really anger me inside but I understood how it had developed and I had to "try" and cut the cancer out.

After the first seven matches I felt things were starting to click but I was in for a big shock. We played away to Heywood St. James and we got hammered 8-1. It was a wakeup call as the attitude of the lads was terrible, and I learnt more about individual players in that match than the whole of the previous season. When we went in the dressing room it was the worst feeling I had ever had, and I knew I had a lot of hard work to do to reassure the lads I was the right man.

Over the next few training sessions I did the bleep test to get the fitness levels up and asked a good mate and an ex-pro Ally Pickering to do a few sessions. These went down really well and we were constantly getting 20 players a session and I could tell the players enjoyed it just looking at the smiles.

Over the next 22 games we only lost one match and were just one point off winning the league title. We lost the title to a team called Chapel Town near Hazel Grove who we beat 4-1 in the last two months of the season. We had played all our games so it was decided in a game Chapel played against Monton Amateurs. If both teams drew we won the league, if one won the winners took the title. We (Avro) were on 63 points, Monton on 61 points and Chapel Town were on 62 but we had superior goal difference so a draw was perfect for us. Scully and me attended the game and the whole town was out on a sunny red-hot Saturday. The crowd was easily over 300 and most of them were rat-arsed and singing their heads off.

Monton took the lead and looked to be well in control, till in the 75th minute Chapel Town equalised. Scully and me just looked at each other...."buzzing" we could read each other's minds. From where I was stood I could see the delegation from the FA putting our clubs coloured ribbons on the trophy, then the Monton goalkeeper made a howler of a save and Chapels right winger slots home from the edge of the box.... Scully and me looked at each other speechless ..... "ill". The place went mental, we just smiled at each other as we walked round to collect the runners up trophy. I congratulated both managers and my heart went out to the Monton manager whose team had been up there all season but now had not even been promoted. He was a fairly old chap who I talked to twice when we played them and he just had an aura about him that told me he was a total football man. I watched him and studied his warm ups before our matches and the way he spoke to his players and the respect he got back. It's something weird that has just stuck with me that I now "try" and blueprint when I talk to players.

As we drove the long drive home I spoke to Scully in depth about the season and I was more than proud of what we had achieved. In the beginning we both would have took tenth place never mind second, we had felt basically no one had given us a chance with the players we had recruited. Edgy, Rob Wood, Martin Moran, Cunny, Tony N, Ryan Shaunnessy, Chris Faulkner, Fitzy, Dave Thornton, Liam Wood, Jimmy McGowan, Killer (Gorton) Dale Cook, Michael McGloughlin (Boggle), Ryan Cook, Nico White, Eric Murphy(?) Rolo, Kyle Wallwork, Kelvin White and last but not least Steve Gavin had all stuck by me and done a job and it was probably the proudest moment we had in football so far. They were a team with all different strengths and weaknesses but moulded into a great team who went on the craziest unbeaten run to end up 5 minutes from winning the title. The Manchester League was 9 divisions lower than the Premiership in the football pyramid, and for the first time in my life I felt I had overcome the odds.

The current manager now is a mate called Rob Fuller and given time he will get it right, of that I have no doubt as he is a committed man.

Avro FC is a fantastic set-up and like many local clubs they produce many quality players so if you get the opportunity to play for them then take it with both hands, it's a place where players who have been released by pro clubs can re-discover their love for football, play local and under no pressure. That's what "Real" football is about.... playing for the love of the game.

The amateur game is going through a major upheaval at the moment due *to the lack of facilities all over the country. The way forward is 4G pitches.*

CHAPTER 8

"MUNICH AND MANCHESTER"

Chapter tune
John Lennon - Imagine

I don't have to write about the events that occurred when the Munich Air Disaster happened in 1958, but what I do want to talk about is the rivalry and hatred that exists between the two Manchester club's fans due to the use of this word.

I cannot speak or represent everyone's feelings on this subject as I do not represent every Manchester City fan. The only thing I can, and want to do is give you my honest opinion and my truthful opinion.

Not once in any book I have ever read has this topic been discussed, maybe because of fear and the fact that it involves the loss of human life in a tragedy. After attending the Munich anniversary Derby I could not write this book without discussing it.

As a young lad in the Kippax in the early 80's anyone will tell you it did not need explaining to you what a "Munich" was. It was sang in nearly every song involving United and it was a reference that was used at City way before I started attending. City fans related it to United the club, and United the fans.

(For an example of where I'm coming from it was like a word we Failsworth lads use to describe Oldhamer's - BIFFO's - Big Ignorant Fookers From Oldham) it was a tag that was attached to United fans and it's club way before many City fans can even remember. So it was installed already and everyone just used it because they knew it really got United fans going and got them pissed off.

Now before I go into it deeper I will start by telling you I have sung songs using the word and I have written songs using the word Munich, so let that be known. When I have sang those songs with many thousands of City fans we sang them in jest, yes jest, to try and take the piss out of United fans about them losing one of the best teams they ever had and get them going.

No excuse I hear you say, "it's still sick and a disgrace to the memory of the members of the team and their families!" Well yes you're correct, it is no excuse and this is not one, but I want to go deeper. As you grow older and wiser and learn about life you realise how precious life is and what it means. At one stage in our lives we have all mocked death in jokes, all been told sick jokes and all had jokes about our mothers and sisters. Not exactly funny I know, but when you're told one you just go uuuuuhhh and know it's not really meant to insult you personally. I believe the mentality of City fans when they sing those songs is not directed at the families or the memories of that bunch of young lads. I believe it's directed at the change it brought to Manchester United and the success that came with it, and I truly believe that.

Something happened at the 2008 Munich Anniversary Game that restored my faith in this theory and I will explain why in this short story.

I have not missed a City v United derby for over 16 years, home and away, and due to me losing interest in watching the game and doing Saturday amateur football and now not attending a lot, this was going to be the first one I ever missed.

I remember being sat at home the day before the game, and all I had been reading about all week was the fact that both clubs were worried that the minute's silence would be broken. Sky Sports would do a daily story on it every day, and I really believe that no one including our own MCFC had any faith in the fans doing it. I was getting a gut feeling I had to go, a weird feeling I had to be there, it was doing my head in for hours, and it was like a voice in my head saying "You can't miss this, it's going to be special... you've got to go"

City tickets for the game were going for crazy money and United tickets were probably the same so I had no chance of getting a ticket even if I wanted to go. The feeling just plagued me for hours and my head was pickled. Finally I picked up the phone and rang "Rozzi" a lad from the Bluewatch supporters group I had set up, he said I had no chance. I was a bit disappointed but I honestly did not expect to get one anyway. Then I'm sat down and I get a text "Phone Paul, Baz isn't going he's got one spare" I was buzzing, my heart was pounding, as a football fan reading this you know exactly the feeling I'm talking about. I phoned Paul straight away and he promised me he would save it for me so I drove to his house on the other side of Manchester at 10pm, I might as well have had the golden ticket for Willie Wonkers Chocolate factory in my hand.

A few of the old brigade got wind I had a ticket and were arranging to all travel together so as to not get sniped. A lot of City fans were expecting a big reception from United's men in black, but I just was not interested.

Part of the bargain was I was to go shopping with the Mrs in the morning, so I did the deed. Mandy wanted to go to Oldham, but was really pushing the boat out in getting there on time. As we travelled up Oldham Road I saw a few City fans who I knew stood at the taxi rank, "Pull over Mandy", "Why" she asked, "Listen love you know this is the biggest game...I got to go" She just put her head against the steering wheel. "I swear I won't get in any trouble - on my kids lives". I pecked her on the cheek, kissed my daughter and bolted from the car. I waved at my mate Chris Harrop and the other lads and jumped in their taxi. They just started laughing their heads off, I did not need to put in words to them what I had just done, they had just probably done the same thing!

We went for a few beers on Salford Quays with about 15 straight going City lads and I just decided to make my way to the ground. I was well known as being a City face by most of United's lads and knew if I walked up Matt Busby Way the chance of one seeing me with 15 lads would provoke a row that I was no longer interested in. Plus the lads I was drinking with would cop for loads of shit they were not prepared for.

As soon as I got to the ground I was pulled aside off the police, searched and held. I could see a few United looking at all of the commotion as they asked me for my ticket. I just played their game and behaved normal, as any fan would do. I did not recognise any as football Intelligence and was confident I would get in. As they let me walk to the turnstile one shouted at me

"Best behaviour Mr Cooper we will be watching you and the rest of your lot" Just shows you, I had not been an active lad for years, but coppers who I had never seen before recognised me, they now obviously get briefed about every football lad! I just ignored them and walked to the turnstile. Due to the commotion with the old bill the stewards made a point of searching me and being total idiots, pulling me out of the queue and patting me down about three times. After five minutes I was in and I just sat on my seat which was at the back near the corporate boxes relieved I was finally there. I picked up my blue and white scarf from the seat and read the note attached talking about Frank Swift and what the day was about.

After 5 minutes I decided to go down to the bar to get a pint and bumped into a good friend Martin Travis and had a chat with him. I will never forget the feeling amongst the City fans that day till I die. Lads were going around shouting to everyone..."Lets show these bastards who we are.......we're not scum" "Lets do the minutes silence, prove everyone wrong"

It was weird, I felt like every blue had the same gut feeling as me, something special was going to happen. You could feel an aura about the place, within the fans, and it was real as though you could touch it. I've never experienced anything like it at a football match in my life. Shouts went up again, "If we do it we will win I just know it, trust me"

It was as if everyone was possessed or had become church preachers. These were City fans I had known and seen at the match for years, some had been fighting lads, some had been lads that I never ever thought would respect the minutes silence. I knew then that there was a time and place for respect and this was it, and every City fan I know in that ground felt exactly the same way as me. It was a disaster that not only affected Manchester United and the players' families, it affected Manchester.

As Mancunians we live with fellow Mancunians who are United fans. Most of our friends from work, or in the pub and most neighbours, relations or family who we love. This is a FACT. The Munich songs in the past were sang, but today I knew all of Manchester was going to pay respect.

As I sat back in my seat I looked at all the United fans and you could feel them looking at the away end waiting to hear the first words of "Who's that lying on the runway" or some similar song. It wasn't going to happen, I just prayed one idiot did not ruin it for everyone else during the silence. A piper led the players on and it was surreal to see the full ground waving scarves, the atmosphere reminded me of the derby's in the 80's and 90's, I felt like I was going back in time. It was without doubt the best derby atmosphere at O.T since the 1-1 game when Ian Brightwell "wellied in" an equaliser past Jim Leighton. City had 8000 that day, and it felt like 8000 this day. The players took up their positions and stood around the centre circle after Sven and Ferguson laid their wreaths on the kick off spot.

"ssssssssssshhhhhhhhhhhhhhh"

"ssssssssssshhhhhhhhhhhhhhh"

The tension was unreal, "Come on city", blues encouraging blues to commit to just one minute in their lives while the announcer declared the minute's silence.

The referee blew.

Can silence ever be heard when 76,000 people are stood next to each other in a 500 yard proximity? I can't put into words what I felt that day, I looked at the surviving players stood on the pitch, Albert Scanlon who had worked with my Gran at Colgate Palmolive on Ordsall Lane in Salford for years, Bobby Charlton who me and mad blue Peter Tranter had met and talked to when we fitted a water meter at his accountant's house. These were people of Manchester who I knew of and my family knew of, some of my family idolised them, yet I had mocked their friends' deaths for years singing and writing songs about a plane crash killing a bunch of young lads and a City legend Frank Swift.

I was running Avro's football team at the time and it ran through my head in that minute how I would feel as their manager if it had been them, so young, with so much of their lives to look forward to, some with kids.

Since I had been involved in amateur football I had been learning how passionate about the game you can become. It had taught me a lot and I felt I had an understanding of a 100th of what was going through Bobby Charlton and Albert Scanlon's hearts.

I looked around the ground as the seconds ticked away, could we make it to 60 seconds with no songs or no snide remarks. I thought to myself, is the ref going to risk the full 60 seconds or what? I watched as 76,000 scarves were held aloft in the air, United fans nervously stood in disbelief - we were doing it.

They were staring at us, we were staring back, I was going - I was getting a lump in my throat?? Yes me the "Munich" singer for 20 years plus, the lad who had fought United fans toe to toe for years, who had hurled abuse at them over terraces, spat on them, punched them, fought them.

Come on...Come on.. blow the whistle I was saying in my head, what are you doing ref. It seemed like an eternity. Exactly at the moment the whistle blew a City fan shouted "COME ON CIIIITY" His timing was perfect, he must have had a stopwatch, no doubt about it. The whole ground clapped and cheered, City fans went mad like they had just won the league, I just looked at Chris Harrop who was stood behind me, "I knew it, I knew we would do it" I was full of emotion, and waved my fist in the air.

Alex Ferguson, the Munich survivors, the City players and even the United players clapped towards the City fans. Even United fans were clapping towards us, I don't care what anyone says, the media, the clubs, the players, nobody believed we would do it. Even I had my doubts, as you know the saying in Manchester, "There's always one isn't there" Well on this occasion not one, not one City fan made a sound.

The game is irrelevant in this story, but we won and got 6 points for the first time in many years. It was the first time I had ever seen us win at O.T and the City fans that day were unreal, the atmosphere was electric. Strangely though United fans were not there usual self and it was a really strange feeling.

I don't believe they thought we could do it, and it definitely affected the fans, which I believe affected the players. United did not play crap that day, it was just that City's players had an extra zip about them and I believe that came from the minutes silence and the fans. At the final whistle we all went mad, and it turned out to be a perfect day and one that changed my outlook on life.

When I say football is powerful, this is exactly what I mean. That day it changed me and I believe 75,000 football fans for the better. It was something that we need to learn from and try and bottle and use again. I've described football as a tool in this book and you may get an idea where I am coming from when you have read it in full. I will probably get slated for writing my true feelings on the "Munich" subject from certain City and United fans. The thing is I don't claim to represent the views of every City and United fan in the things I have written in this book. The only thing we all have in common is that we are football fans, I have my opinions and everyone has a right to theirs.

There is a chance that the mentality of many football fans will change and the "Munich" chants will be replaced with a song that was sung on that special day.........."We are Impeccable".

It is so easy to get caught up into the pride of the game and see it evolve into hate. This I believe is where we all need to learn to balance the positives and negatives of the game to feel the full energy.

CHAPTER 9

"FOOTBALL" FOR LIFE

The next three chapters of this book I am going to go into the title, some people who know me say I go too deep sometimes in everything I do, a lot of the time it makes people laugh, it makes people angry and it makes people cry.

As you read the book you will come to make your own decision if it's for the best or for the worst. No matter what you think I'm not going to change as that's me like it or lump it.

I often think why it was football that took a grip of me when I was never particularly outstanding as a player. I was the lad who was always picked last or "near" last when we played in school break times and the full year was up against the wall waiting for the chosen captain to pick his players.

As we all know footballs a game played with a round sphere called a ball, and the idea is to get the ball in the net with your feet and score a goal working as a team to achieve the final result, making you victorious after 90 minutes of play. Part of this game is that you must stick to the rules and regulations to be successful when playing so it is a fair contest.

On the playing side I personally think what attracts kids to play is the fact that anyone on that pitch can become the hero and win his/her team the game by the way they play, their attitude or possibly their leadership qualities. If we go back to our school days, as soon as you got that ball at your feet you wanted to kick it as hard as you could and pray it went in the goal so you could run around the yard celebrating. Many times this will have ended with your team mates chasing you to jump all over you and give you the adulation of being a 20 second hero.

On the negative side, you could miss a tackle and let the opposition through to score an equalising goal to become the villain all within 60 seconds. That, I believe is the pull factor in football and why so many of us are addicted to it. If we want examples of how unpredictable football can become we only have to think of three games...

The FA Cup final in the 80's between Liverpool and Wimbledon, when the Womble's shocked the world by winning 1-0.

Manchester City's play-off final against Gillingham at Wembley in 1999 when they were dead and buried but came back and won on penalties.

Man United's comeback in the European Cup final against Bayern Munich in the same year when they came from behind to win 2-1 after being 1-0 down for the duration of the game. They scored in the last five minutes of game play to win the competition which made it one of the most memorable finals ever.

The feeling for all sets of fans involved in those games is that powerful it is impossible to put into words. It's the feeling of being on the edge of defeat one second, and on the verge of victory the next.   Like you all, I've felt it in the school yard, on the grass pitches of amateur football and in the stadiums where City have played. More recently I've felt it watching football on Sky Sports.

I cannot think of another world team sport where emotions and feelings can change so quickly. The sport is that powerful I truly think we as a human race underestimate how influential it can be on our societies and also us as people.

Feelings are that passionate about it, on the negative side it has caused hooligan firms across the world to be born, which has resulted in death and even wars. (Yugoslavia, South America) It has also changed people's lives in the fact that it has divided families and friendships and in some cases even marriages.

When I think about the above I know deep down it is not the sport called "Football" that has caused this. I believe it is something which has attached itself to the game and people in general have naturally attached to the game, one word........PRIDE.

I once listened to a talk by a man I respect very highly, he described pride as a dangerous thing. For years it baffled me even after I had listened to him speak for over thirty minutes on the subject. Over the years though I have, as we all have, studied life and how we as a human race react. Whether it be a fight in the street, an argument between girls in a pub or a war on the television "pride" is involved in all these things at one point or another. To go deeper just have a look at what I found in the dictionary for the word "Pride"

1. The quality or state of being proud; inordinate self-esteem; an unreasonable conceit of one's own superiority in talents, beauty, wealth, rank, etc., which manifests itself in lofty airs, distance, reserve, and often in contempt of others.

2. A sense of one's own worth, and abhorrence of what is beneath or unworthy of one; lofty self-respect; noble self-esteem; elevation of character; dignified bearing; proud delight; -- in a good sense.

3. Proud or disdainful behaviour or treatment; insolence or arrogance of demeanour; haughty bearing and conduct; insolent exultation; disdain. .

4. That of which one is proud; that which excites boasting or self-gratulation; the occasion or ground of self-esteem, or of arrogant and presumptuous confidence, as beauty, ornament, noble character, children, etc.

6. Highest pitch; elevation reached; loftiness; prime; glory; as, to be in the pride of one's life.

Read it again and think about it for five minutes before you read on.

Makes you think a bit doesn't it?? To be honest I think pride is like anything in life, in moderation and used in the right way its good for everyone, however used in a large quantity it can be very dangerous.

One of the greatest things about football is nobody can ever predict a result and be 100 percent sure of it. Yes we can have the favourites but everybody, including myself loves the underdog.

As I write this book in the month of July in 2009, player's wages are soaring to the dizzy height of over 150 grand a week. The working class game born out of factories and churches has turned into a worldwide game surrounded by media frenzy. Football fans all over the world have different opinions on whether the game is healthy or just an industry for greedy men who put nothing back in the game. People predict that the bubble will burst, and that it will have to come back down to earth with a bang.

On a personal note, at this time in my life it is irrelevant to me if it does or doesn't, because all I know is that the game itself will never die no matter what. I as well as many others have enjoyed watching grassroots football as much as watching the world cup finals, and this is the beauty of the game that gives it an eternal foundation.

All you need for football to survive is a ball, nothing else on the planet motivates us more than looking at a ball. The game was played on cobbled streets by players such as Bobby Charlton, Jimmy Greaves, George Best, Colin Bell and we now even know it exists in those places still, as we see it first hand wherever we go around the world.

As I sit writing this in a hotel room in the Dominican Republic (whose first sport is baseball) I only have to put the TV on to see there are five channels in three different languages all dedicated to football. The game has never been so healthy globally and you can understand why sponsorship throws so much money at the game.

Personally, like a lot of people I believe the money coming in to the game should be filtering down to the grassroots game more. I once attended an FA grassroots meeting at the City Of Manchester Stadium where Trevor Brooking the ex-West Ham and England star was in attendance. He came across as a great football man who seemed very humble and had a great attitude to grassroots football. When he stood up and spoke his words that evening they hit me really hard and shocked me. He was basically coming across to the audience that his hands were tied and that the FA would have to look at being restructured for the money to filter through to grassroots football like it should do. This was over 3 years ago and it really made me think about how passionate he was about the game, yet he was still so annoyed and frustrated at the ignorance the game was receiving from the top to the bottom at grassroots level.

Since that meeting though I have seen slow improvements of facilities where I live in Manchester. The borough of Oldham though is sadly lagging behind and is deteriorating faster than it is progressing in my opinion. This is I believe due to the bad-management of its current facilities and its co-operation with local amateur football clubs. Many of its sites are running at a loss and the maintenance of its grass pitches are becoming a burden and not cost effective so they are selling them off after leaving them over grown and unattended. This is the same with many borough councils across the country and the reason why thousands of kid's football teams are struggling for pitches.

Football is more popular than it has ever been at the moment and especially junior and women's football. There are more qualified coaches than there has ever been, and there are more kids involved from all backgrounds than ever before. The main problem with football is that participation levels are outgrowing the available facilities. This is a nationwide problem and it is not going to go away until the government, local authorities and the FA work with each other in a quicker manner. If this does not happen very soon many amateur teams will start to turn kids away, and these kids will end up doing other things that may not benefit society.

On the coaching and player side, I personally do not believe the amateur game has been in a better condition ever. Any woman or man in this country has the opportunity to join a local charter standard club and be put through their FA coaching badges for free. Many thousands of coaches have done this and this has, and will continue to produce better home-grown players for our national team given time.

I speak to a lot of old managers and players who talk about the amateur teams of the past saying that they would hammer today's teams if they were to play each other. I totally disagree as when I watch today's amateur football I watch many teams that train two evenings a week and do twenty minute warm ups before games. I also see amateur managers doing more structured coaching under floodlit facilities at night, I see amateur managers using class rooms for technical training and PowerPoint sessions. Many players I see studying coaching DVD's at home in their front room feasting upon the words of professional coaches. Technically, I do not believe the game has ever been in a stronger position in its coaching values like I said the final piece of the jigsaw is more facilities and more support for these community clubs and it's members.

Many great standards have filtered down from the top of the game to grassroots but sadly the money has yet to follow. Women's football is the fastest growing sport in the country as I speak, yet the ladies team I have been coaching have been unsuccessful in finding a local pitch to compete in the open age ladies league. I do not doubt this is the same all over the country and especially in the urban and inner city areas of England. All we can do as a population of football though is to keep raising our voices and fighting for every blade of grass we can for the future of the grassroots game in this country. Things are improving but if voices stay silent then actions of the authorities stand still.

I believe the most difficult problem today's modern amateur coach has is the attitude of many parents. I see so many young players with great talent and potential that is destroyed by their parent's personal ambitions. Many mums and dads see there child as a golden goose and dream of them becoming the next David Beckham or Wayne Rooney. This becomes purely motivated by the thinking of the money and the possibilities of a different lifestyle and way of living for them as well as their child, this then has a negative impact on the child as great expectation is loaded upon him/her. The child then either becomes as possessed as their parent and does not absorb any instructions from the coach or team mate, or becomes confused as he/she has two sources of information conflicting in their brain. This is where I believe the child's love of the game dies over time and where we lose so many great talents.

A manager once said to me that a player is the mirror image on a pitch as he is off it. That is something that is now gospel doctrine in my knowledge of being a football manager and I have proved it to myself over the last few years.

If a player is a "flash harry" off the pitch and is full of self-vanity you can guarantee he is not a team player on the pitch, he is just about his own game. If a player in his day job, works all the over-time offered to him he will be a grafter on the pitch who works hard for his team.

If a player has problems respecting authority (parents) or the law off the pitch he will constantly be getting booked and sent off on it.

If a player has bad time keeping or finances at home he will bring it to your team.

If a player does the minimum in his day job for the minimum wage he has to survive, he will do exactly the same on the pitch.

If a player is unstable in his relationship with his partner he will go from club to club for his whole career. He will never be happy.

If you want to judge a player before he kicks a ball, look at the people he hangs out with away from the game. That will tell you everything, as people only surround themselves with people who they admire. FACT

I could go on for two pages but I think you might get the idea of where I am coming from. This does not mean these players are useless, far from it! It just highlights the areas you have to work on more to get them performing to their full potential. That is the work a coach and especially a manager should be striving to do. In my opinion there is no greater achievement in management as seeing a player improve that has been rejected off another club or team. You can have all the trophies you want as a manager but the biggest trophy is seeing an ex-player who was once a menace to society and himself, walking down the street with his family showing love and respect to his community. If you are an amateur manager you will know exactly where I am coming from in saying that statement, and this is one of the things that keeps my hunger for the game alive. I am sure many people look at me walking down the road with my kids and think the same thing. Without a doubt football has improved my outlook on life and given me great friends as well as an education on people. It's taught me many things in life that have helped me in my personal life, and this is something that I want to share. Its one of the main reasons I am writing this book as I feel I owe it back to the game that has given me so much.

CHAPTER 10

"LIFE"

Chapter tunes
Oasis - Masterplan -
Johnny Cash Gods gonna cut you down

Well done, you've reached Chapter 10 and by now I bet your head is full of mixed emotions. A bit like watching a football match not knowing what the outcome will be till the final whistle is blown. They say that football is the game of god, and I totally agree. It represents every thing he is trying to achieve with us as individuals while we have this short stay in this life.

As we age we realise life is very short and very precious, and the most important factor is that every minute we breathe the air, we are "learning". Exactly the same as playing, managing or even watching a football match. Without a shadow of a doubt this beautiful game has improved peoples lives by bring them together and taking down barriers by teaching us we are all the same. Like anything it can be used as a positive or a negative, and we as a human race have to balance its competitive edge by making sure pride does not over take humility in competition.

The greatest sight on a football pitch in my opinion is a player pulling up an opposition player to his feet by the hand. It's a sign of respect and an example how we as a people can help each other in life. When some one is down you make sure you put a hand out to help because one day it will be you on the floor looking for someone to pull you up. It does not matter on your colour, the language you speak or where you come from. We can all help each other while we compete in life or even in a game of football.

As a former manager I feel it is a vital part of the process to taste defeat so that when you taste victory you know the difference and what is needed work wise to attain that status, exactly the same in our personal lives. How can we improve in life if we as individuals do not make mistakes?

There are many times in football when we have seen a starting 11 of the best technical individual players lose to a "team" of lesser players who work harder and are organised. Teamwork is the key to the game and usually it consists of a mix of all different players with totally different attributes in age as well as ability.

Sir Alex Ferguson has been the best manager at this for two decades of my life and at times as much as I hate watching his team's success, I admire how he builds a team. He will have his flair players, his workhorses, his players with great defensive abilities but the key ingredient he installs in them is teamwork and a will to work for each other no matter what the score or the situation.

You play to the final whistle and do your duty as a member of that team to the max. If you fail and cannot adapt to his squads standards and application and want to be independent you are out the door. This is successful at the highest standard of football in the world.

On the other side of the fence in grassroots football we can use the gift of the game by installing moral standards into our children and even adults that will become vital tools for them in the future. If you are a player, coach or even a manager you will know this pays dividends if applied correctly and used with patience.

Respect is the key word in football that is used in reference at the moment in the way players talk to and respond to referee's. I believe this should be the motto and word used by the world of football in everything it tries to achieve. Many players I have managed over the years do not respect themselves and that I believe is the first hurdle in installing morals and values within a person or player. As human beings we are born all the same as miniature sponges absorbing everything in around us. Life dictates that we do not choose our surroundings or families yet usually this dictates the personality we become. Over time though we all learn we can change that and progress on our own if we choose to do so.

This is why life and football are so beautiful, as no two people or players are the same. We all have the ability to improve and change if we want to listen to our peers or coaches. Many times we can listen to the wrong ones but the key is still to listen and show respect to authority as we can make our own decision over time, which was right or wrong.

Football has taught me many things in life and without it I would not be the person I am today. I have made a lot of mistakes and a lot of wrong decisions but they have made me grow as a person and a human being. A wise man once told me "a mistake is only a mistake if you do it again". Many times in my life as we all have, I have known I am doing wrong and thought I could get away with it. Then out of the blue and totally unexpected I have been punished for it and felt a fool. No more though so than in amateur football although luckily for me I have not let those experiences repeat in my personal life, as the game has been the experiment for me.

As a person I feel I have no excuse, as I had a decent family life compared to some friends I know who had it really tough. A lot of times I feel I have let a lot of people down over life like we all do.

My worst regret was getting involved in drugs at an early age, which took me down some dark paths in my life. The first drug I fell for was cigarettes, and I can remember the day I fell to the temptation of inhaling a fag just to look good, it was that cool it made me violently sick, but after a while I forced my body to accept it and thought to myself all my parents warning words were a load of rubbish.

From cigarettes I went to alcohol, weed, pills and eventually cocaine, which would eventually nearly destroy my life. I often wonder where my life would be if I had not had that first cigarette, as the cigarette opened the other doors to further my addictions that would lead me down paths leading me away from the positive aspects of football to which I loved in my school years.

As you have read I went down the football hooligan road, which comes hand in hand with cocaine, alcohol and the addiction of violence. Many times at the match we were drug fuelled which led to arrests which then led to girlfriends or wives and children distressed and employment lost due to time off work.

Like everyone I put my family second to my life of drugs, which I hid from many friends and my family for over 20 years. Cocaine is a wolf in sheep's clothing as it is socially acceptable in today's society and is classed as a champagne drug. If you did not have it on the club circuit or football hooligan scene then there was seriously something wrong with you.

For me, my cocaine days started when I became mixed up in selling drugs and involved in the club scene and the Madchester rave days. It started by selling ecstasy and weed from the age of sixteen. This then got to a point where I was making lots of money and made myself and my mates an attractive outlet for cocaine dealers. Cocaine was pretty rare in the Madchester days of the early 90's but by 1995/96 it was becoming more available and easier to sell as more and more of the old school ravers were moving on from ecstasy tablets to a bag of cocaine for the night's entertainment. In ten years from 1991 an ecstasy tablet went from the price of £20 to just £2 and became a poor mans drug.

For the drug dealer it was a dream come true as you could double your profits by simply cutting it with any white powder and flogging it for the same price. There was no other drug on the market that could and still can make you so much money so fast.

People never complained about how strong it was and very rarely asked for their money back so it was a ticket to print money. I witnessed many times a kilo of cocaine getting blended with a kilo of white powder which came in many forms such as Novocaine, Creatine, Paracetamel and many other chemicals that came straight out of the front or sometimes back door of a chemist.

As dealers we would keep our own personal pure coke and sell the bashed up powder in ounces for the same price we got the pure. The lads we were giving it to were clueless and were just happy to make a few hundred quid a week while me and my click made a few grand.

To cut a long story short over time we began mixing and dealing with people that were way out of our league. I was witnessing brutal tactics and the other lads were mixing and getting involved with people from across Europe. It is a part of my life that I wish to remain closed and I do not even discuss with my family or close friends.

It's something I just do not discuss with anyone anymore. These are things I have to live with that have scarred me for life and I continue to live with the guilt of the things I got involved with and the actions I carried out.

Over the years I have realised what a good decision it was to move away from those circles as many of my friends have gone to prison doing long time, and some have even lost their lives to drug dealing and everything that surrounds it. Over time I have seen good friends turn on each other and end up being enemies to such a degree where lives have nearly been taken and people destroying each other for purely greed.

I remember one lad asking me how many people actually make a great life for themselves out of selling drugs. The answer that was given is irrelevant because over time I have learnt it is 0.

I have never met a person who has a happy family life with kids well brought up, who is selling or involved in drug dealing. You reap what you sow and no matter what you will always come unstuck eventually. There will be a few people reading this who beg to differ but if the drug does not get you the world will, it's only a matter of time.

You may get ten or twenty years of a lavish lifestyle if you are very lucky, but I guarantee you even if you get that far you will sit on your bed counting your money realising there is something missing. You will look back at what you sacrificed and lost to get yourself in that position and eventually you will put your head in your hands. As you get older you will have sleepless nights constantly looking over your shoulder and twitching at the curtains when you hear the slightest noise. This frame of mind then builds a prison around you and your home will have to become a fortress, as you will trust nobody. This is the path some people choose and then announce that they have a great life. To me it's a life of prison, which eventually leads to mental torment and grief.

Every human being on this planet has good or bad within them and we all choose our own paths. I believe every person born into this world is born good and it is only the world that turns us into bad given the chance.

I still have many great friends who are involved in drugs, and to some people that may seem a horrible thing to say and I totally understand. The thing is over time I have learnt that people can change and you need to sit back sometimes and let people learn the hard way, if you are a good friend you make sure you are there for them when they fall. I have found in my life it is vital not to judge anyone no matter of their appearance, colour of skin, religion or what they practice. Easier said than done I know, but a vital key to life that we can all use.

I don't condone what they do, but in my eyes the man who sells cigarettes and alcohol to kids is as much danger to society as the cocaine dealer. The only way to beat drugs is to educate our children about the dangers of all addictive substances, because no matter what society does they will only go away if we give kids another option to use their time. I have promised to myself to be as open as possible about my mistakes being involved in drugs so then hopefully my children will choose wiser paths. The key is not making them scared or ashamed to ask me!

Even though I stopped being involved in the selling of drugs I was unable to kick the habit of mixing in the circles of friends who took the drug. By the time the millennium came round 80 percent of my friends were users and it was impossible to go out on a night out and not have it offered to you.

Many times I would sneak home at three o clock in the morning and sit up all night staring at the ceiling with my jaw swinging, totally wired, thinking deep thoughts about depressing aspects of my life. Don't get me wrong, this did not happen over night, it took 15 years for me to start realising I had a problem, as I never wanted to admit I was addicted to cocaine.

How could I be addicted to cocaine? I only had it on a Friday and a Saturday! It's like saying you don't smoke because you only smoke at weekends. The fact of the matter is you are programming your body to accept drugs as fuel every weekend, and let me tell you as soon as you get paid on Friday your sub-conscious is telling you 11 digits on a phone and how to get your hit.

Many of you reading this will be thinking it will never happen to me! Well let me tell you if you are, you are the favourite to become addicted and having a life of hell. It will come into your life like a thief in the night, and have you on your knees, as it is not a respecter of any form of man or woman on this planet. If you want proof just attend a Narcotics Anonymous meeting where you will see lawyers, celebrities, nurses, doctors and even politicians pouring their hearts out for help and understanding. Mentally it will twist your mind into depression and bring your body into a lazyitis mode that will change your personality and make you volatile to people you love dearly. When you are on the drug it drops you morals and you have no sense or fear of doing wrong, whether it be violence or doing something that would break a loved ones heart. Cocaine increases the sex drive but with it comes the loss of the feeling of love replaced with the feeling of dirt. The drug naturally makes you put the fear of consequence to the back of your mind and urges you to lust after anything of the opposite sex.

If the devil has materials for a house of destruction and hell for man, then this is his sand and cement for his foundations and brickwork. At your work place you will become lazy and carefree and have no motivation to fulfil your role you will start having a lot of time off work sick and sleeping long sleeps and eating more through this pattern. It is only now through being cocaine and alcohol free have I started to realise how this drug has had such a huge negative impact on my life.

You may be saying what has this to do with football? Well for me it has everything to do with football because football was a major impact in me curing my addictions. The strange thing is I never expected it to do it in the way it did and at the time it did.

I had been doing amateur football for six years as a manager and in 2008 I was running the reserve team at Failsworth Dynamos as a favour for my friend Wayne Kennedy who I highly respected as a manager and still do. The team consisted of about 19 lads all ranging from ages from 16 to 26 from a lot of different backgrounds. It was a mixture of lads I had brought in from past teams and young lads who had played for local kids teams and who now wanted to make the next step up to senior football.

We started off fantastic and were top of the league for the first seven games and things looked well. Then overtime for one reason or another I lost a few lads through injuries and a few loose arguments and discipline issues where I failed to admit I got it wrong. I lost many key experienced players and was having to field four young lads 18 and under and their confidence was getting lower as we were getting beat week after week.

During this time I was using cocaine, unknown to the club committee and my family every Friday night. This then put me in the wrong frame of mind on a Saturday and I was losing my patience and making bad mistakes due to my head being all over the place with family issues I was creating due to my cocaine addictions.

Then one Saturday I was on the toilet in the changing rooms when I heard a few players talking about the fact that they had seen me 'coked up' the night before in the local pub. I knew this was common knowledge to a few of them, but I was devastated that the young players had learnt about it. How the hell could I expect my players to produce on a Saturday and at training knowing their manager was only an example of how to be a coke head?

It made me think like I had never thought before, I thought about how much of a failure I had been as a manager and most importantly as a husband and a father. I thought of my two daughters finding out through their friends and how people really perceived me. It took me back to my wedding night and how the next day I was opening wedding cards with bags of cocaine inside them. Mandy would try and flush them down the toilet in disgust while I was trying to see how pure the coke was.

I was 37 years of age and had been using cocaine for 17 years even though I had been diagnosed with a leaking heart valve. I had still carried on even after the birth of my daughter Millie and I had sat warning my eldest daughter Cherelle about the dangers of drugs even though I was still using them. All in all I realised I was a total disgrace and a failure at that point in my life. So guess what I did? I got some more cocaine to make me feel better and sat in the pub talking utter crap with my cocaine buddies for five hours!

After leaving the pub at two o clock in the morning, reality started to hit home and I was going into depressed mode again thinking about the mess my life was in and where it all went wrong. I hid all my worries from my family and sat in bed sweating thinking deeper and deeper about how much of a mess I was in. I was embarrassed to be a husband, a father and most of all to call myself a man.

I sat and thought about all the problems the drug had brought into my life even though over the years I thought I was invincible. The more I thought the more depressed I got, the more depressed I got the more I could not sleep, the more I could not sleep the more thinking I did about depressing things. The drug did not seem to be wareing off at all as I tossed and turned scratching my body and wiping the sweat from my forehead.

My thoughts then went to other people's lives who I knew like Anthony Rowan from watching Manchester City. I class him as a great friend of mine, who is suffering really badly from Multiple Sclerosis. His body, as he liked to put it was "goosed" and his life was like a mortal prison as he had to be carried into bed as his muscles had been destroyed by the disease so much he was basically paralysed, yet when I visited him he still smiled and cracked joke after joke about life.

Craig Reed, another lad from the match who was fighting a daily battle with drug and alcohol addiction. Craig is the strongest and fittest lad I know but he struggled with the willpower to beat and cure his addictions. He had lost his home, girlfriend and his job but still phoned me telling me he was never going to give up and try again.

Paul Daniels was another lad I thought of who was doing four years in prison and had lost everything from his family to his job.

These thoughts gave me hope and made me realise how lucky I actually was compared to other people in this world. I thought of the young serving in Iraq and Afghanistan, dodging bullets and watching their mates get blown to pieces in front of their eyes. I realised I did not have it so bad after all, in fact everything I had brought on upon myself and it had just come to a pinnacle.

Then as I looked at my draw cabinet I saw a book my mum had given me years ago as a young teenager. It was a combined copy of the Bible and the Book of Mormon which was always at the side of my bed. I had been brought up a Christian all my childhood and had been taught that we must never forget how to pray as it was our phone to God.

I sat there thinking about my youth and how happy my life had been when I had attended church and had looked after myself by obeying the guidelines of the church's principles. I compared the lives of my friends who had stayed in church and how unaffected they had become by drugs and other addictions through listening to the teachings of the church. If I wanted the perfect example then I only had to look at my brother Louis.

Louis was just a year younger than me, and a great football player who was adored by all his mates. He was a lad who had faced the same obstacles in life as me yet chose to listen to my mum's wisdom and guidance unlike myself.

As a child I wanted to listen to nobody, and just go off what I saw in front of me and see and learn for myself. It was a bit like the tortoise and the hare story with me being the hare. I always wanted to be at the front not looking behind me or even left and right, just straight ahead.

I looked at my family for emergencies and my friends for wisdom, which in hindsight is the worst mistake you can make in life. I thought about how stable his life was as he concentrated solely on family values and being a good person to other people by being a Christian. It still had a great balance and he still enjoyed watching city and playing football as well as getting church involved in community work. His life evolves around his wife and his kids and its something that I knew was a million miles away from where I was.

As I looked at the Bible I thought about praying and asking for help. Then I thought why would god help me? Then I went into depressed mode thinking about how much of a mess I had caused in my life that had affected other people. Strange thing was though the more I thought about it the more I knew I had nothing to lose.

The Christian faith teaches us that god loves all men and will answer his prayers if they ask him in faith believing in Jesus Christ. What had I to lose?

I got up out of bed and went down stairs and got on my knees and prayed. I prayed like I had never prayed before asking for help and comfort and to feel normal. The most important thing I did was to ask for forgiveness and help in turning my life around. After five minutes of praying I went back to bed and nothing happened although I did feel at peace and went to sleep straight away.

When I awoke in the morning I felt groggy and horrible but was determined not to take it out on the kids or the wife so I took the dog for a walk. After thinking more and more about how I needed to change, I decided I had to do it one step at a time. When I returned home I went to my bed and prayed again and read the scriptures.

Even though I read, nothing registered in my head that made any sense so I just kept reading and praying for a week or two. I attended a few Narcotics Anonymous meetings, which really hit home to me how lucky I actually was. I was hearing stories of men and women who had lost everything and things were starting to hit home of how much in the danger zone I actually was. After work I started going on a run with my i-pod listening to music that I had learnt to love throughout my life. It took me back through my rave days and all the dark days. I started staying in at a weekend instead of going straight to the pub on a Friday. The more I stayed in the more I went running listening to my music. The more I did this the more I prayed and asked for answers and for help.

I was feeling different as a person and it was as if my mind was becoming clearer and I was determined I wanted to change. When Sunday came I was tempted to go back to church but I knew it would make my wife start thinking I was crazy and to be honest after all the stuff I had done I did not think myself a really worthy person to be sat in a house of god.

Occasionally my wife Mandy and I would go out as a couple and I would bump into someone in a pub and have a cheeky line in the toilet. Mandy would just look at me in disgust and ask me to swear down that I had not had a line. I would feel ashamed and just tell her lie after lie and then react in anger, which would then ruin the night with us going home early. Again I would be sat up in bed sweating getting depressed and feeling rejected, as Mandy would tell me to keep my hands off her. I would then get out of bed and go downstairs walking up and down the kitchen hating myself for having that drug again. Many times I would literally feel suicidal as I felt I was a prisoner to the drug and could not escape from it.

I would drink pure orange juice and as much liquid as I could to try and get to sleep. Often looking at myself in the mirror thinking how much of a failure and a disgrace I was, I was a 37 year old cocaine addict with two kids, a great wife and a great job throwing it all away and I could see it clear as day but was prepared to do nothing about it.

They say cocaine is not a big killer in relation to drugs but I beg to differ. What society fails to realise is that cocaine is the foundation and fuel for the biggest killer of men under the age of 40. Depression! I have lost a lot of friends who have taken their own lives who were users, but at the funerals no one mentions the fact that the drug was the problem. This is because cocaine is the master of disguise and no family wants to bury their child admitting he/she was a user or an addict. Cocaine is so active in our society it is as acceptable as a cigarette and a pint. There are no clear physical deformities standing a user out from the crowd like heroin does. It's a champagne drug and that's why it is so acceptable. Cocaine does not get to you when you're out in the club or pub, or even on the night you have it. It gets you when you walk through your front door after your night out and then Monday to Friday.

Many users I know call it D mode meaning depression mode, and it's the mental aspect of it that hits home. Only god knows what damage the other chemicals mixed in with it does to your body? Many times I came in from a night out with major stomach pains that would have me in tears and passing blood when I was on the toilet. Other times my nose would bleed constantly or I would struggle breathing to a point where I was gasping for air. The more I write about the affects of the drug the more I realise how much damage I may have done to my body.

I was determined more than ever to stop, even though I kept failing to keep to my own personal promises. I thought about sharing my problem with Mandy, my mum and my dad but I just felt ashamed and I was convinced that I could beat my addiction alone.

I got on my knees again and prayed for help and understanding and asked if there really was a god to show his cards and take away the horrible feelings I had of being wired and depressed. I went back upstairs and I slept as soon as my head hit the pillow.

The following day I gave up on god and just got back to my normal life doing football. I wasn't enjoying it anymore and my enthusiasm for the game was dying, as I felt unworthy of standing in front of the lads and representing such a great amateur football club like Failsworth Dynamos.

On the Monday I sent the committee an e-mail telling them I was resigning for family reasons but would carry on till the end of the season. Dynamos was a family club and I felt I was deceiving everybody by trying to be part of something when the fact was I was a drug addict, the players, the staff and the families of every young kid associated to the club and amateur football in general.

I wanted to concentrate on my family for once. Mandy and the kids had been putting up with me doing football every weekend for the past six years. It was time to put something back and make a major effort in devoting some time with my wife and children as well as curing my addictions.

The following week I was sat in the house when Mandy answered the door to two Mormon missionaries. Mandy let them in and looked at me with her eyebrows raised! For some strange reason she let them sit down and I just froze and let them talk. I was in a state of shock as I knew Mandy was not a religious person and saw no need for god and I knew she was on edge. The missionaries introduced themselves as Elder and Sister Berry and they were an old couple who to be honest were really polite and humble.

As they were sat down I felt good as they talked about the church and the principles of Jesus Christ and how it could have an impact on our family. I still do not know to this day why they knocked on my door at this time in my life but I felt inside I had to go to church to listen and start to find out for myself. I had been asking for strength and help for the last two weeks, maybe this was it? Mandy was not interested but I asked her if it was ok if I went to church, to which see seemed quite shocked. I totally understood her reasons as she sees religion as most people do as a hindrance to life and something that is useless and only starts wars and arguments. Even though, she being the great wife she is has never once stopped me from doing anything I have asked as long as it does not bring misery to the house.

That was fourteen months ago and I have been going ever since. It has caused arguments in my marriage but over time my wife and kids have seen I have changed for the better so it not a problem for me to disappear for a few hours on a Sunday.

In that time I have stopped smoking and using cocaine and not had a drink once. This is something I have tried to do for years but failed time and time again. I spend more time with my family and listen to my wife and kids and all my energy goes into them and my home instead of the pub and my mates. I have had little relapses but still carry on getting up off the floor and starting again. I know I have received the strength to do this by becoming closer to God.

I am not saying that the last fourteen months have been easy, far from it. I have lost a well-paid job and had to take a job with 50 percent less wages, as I was made redundant due to the credit crunch. During this time our family has struggled financially and really had to change our lives and sacrifice things we had took for granted just to pay the bills.

It was during this time we came to realise how much of a financial mess we were actually in. We cut our cloth accordingly and got rid of things like Sky TV and started looking at our income and started living accordingly. I shopped about for cheaper life insurance as well as car insurance. We went through our domestic bills and shopped about for cheaper suppliers. We saved a small fortune and if we would have done this a few years earlier it could easily have paid for a family holiday for two weeks every year.

For ten months we struggled but now I look back it was the best thing that happened to us as a family as it made us humble and realise how much money we were wasting away. After our bills were paid and our food shopping bought we barely had £50 a week to spare for clothes or family days out. I got a job with a company maintaining student accommodation in Rusholme. During that time I had to paint nine flights of stairs in magnolia paint. Painting was something I hated, but it was the job I was paid to do so I did it. I would paint with my iPod and listen to music to get me through the day which gave me a lot of thinking time. I thought a lot about my life and how fast it had gone and the money and time I had wasted away while using cocaine. I also thought about how I could change and convinced myself during this time that it was never two late. My wife and children came to mind a lot of times and realised how ignorant I had been to them as well as my mum and dad and other loved ones.

I would listen to Oasis, Johnny Cash and all the Old Skool house tunes of the Hacienda and relive my youth while painting. Sometimes I would feel that good I would break out in a cheeky dance on the stairs with my iPod blaring down my ears. They say music is good for the spirit and I totally agree, some of the lyrics to Oasis songs really hit home to me and I often wondered how much Noel and Liam Gallagher's catholic upbringing really influenced them. The lyrics of many of their songs still inspire me to this day as I feel I can relate to them so easily.

Over the course of painting those stairs it made me more humble and realise a lot of things about the course of my life. Working round the corner from Tony Rowan (my mate suffering from M.S) I popped round to see him a few times. Sometimes I came out of that flat so inspired that it brought me to tears. Rowan wakes up in a prison everyday and will do for the rest of his life due to the ferocity and destruction this disease has inflicted on his body. When I sit there and listen to him he makes me smile and many a time I have questioned why god would let this happen to a great bloke like Tony. The truth is I do not know, but I do believe that Tony has been a huge influence on me writing this book. If this man can live life in this way for the rest of his days then surely I can do something to help him highlight his pain and the importance of the world finding a cure for this disease?

I have watched Tony's body deteriorate over many years and I do not doubt he is in a living hell for many hours of his life. The lads at the match have raised money for him and many pay personal visits to him regularly to support him the best they can. The one thing that angers me is that for the past few years Tony has been left in a flat in the heart of Moss Side at the back of a boarded up pub. Surely a paralysed man suffering from M.S deserves more support and a better environment to see out the last of his days. Tony is a very proud man and will be angry I am complaining on his behalf, but I am convinced this needs to be highlighted and the disease needs to be made more aware for people.

Tony was like me, a football hooligan at Manchester City but for the last fifteen years he has been facing a bigger battle than any football lad I know. When I think of him or visit him I become ashamed at myself for feeling sorry for my own problems and look at Tony for inspiration. I never mention my religion because if I was in his place it would be the last thing I want to talk about. We talk about City and the old days and what a lot of the lads are up to, but as I write this book I am determined to do something in respect of his daily battle with the disease.

Even though I do not work round the corner anymore I often think of Tony and pray for him a lot. I like many believers in God do not have all the answers to why certain people suffer so much, but I do believe one day Tony will have a fully functional body and live another life and I believe I will see him in that form. I do not have proof but I have a faith and testimony that these things will happen through my own personal revelation.

I believe The Church of Jesus Christ of Latter Day Saints Is the restored church placed upon this earth by God himself for the salvation of all men. I do not expect anyone person to believe me as my life is no example to follow, but I have studied in depth the Bible and The Book of Mormon and I believe it to be true.

I know many of you reading will ask how I know it is true. Well I say to you that I have prayed and asked for answers and the Holy Spirit of God has given me my answers and I know like millions of others that it is true simply because I have asked with all my heart.

I am treated by God no different than any other man or woman upon this planet and I can testify to you that if you do the simple thing of asking with all your heart you will receive the answers you want in this life.

It is something once felt I believe no living man or woman can ever truthfully deny. The first lesson I received was to be made humble and stripped of my pride, which now I look back, was the only way I could move forward. No matter if I fall off the recovery wagon and return to my previous lifestyle I will never deny what I know is true.

In my life nobody upon nobody has ever dictated to me what I should do or paths I should choose. Many people have tried but I have always been the person who has come to my own conclusions.

As you have read, a large percentage of them have been wrong and led me down some dark paths but this time I believe I am right.

Since I have attended church and prayed daily, I have felt inside a cleanness and warmth that I cannot describe. Sometimes it is so pure and beautiful it has had me in tears as it is like no other feeling I have ever encountered.

People will laugh and say I am totally off my rocker and that I am feeling the after affects of coming down off drugs for seventeen years, but as I write these words I swear to you, the reader, if you read the Bible and Book of Mormon for yourself and pray with all your heart and ask the questions, you will receive the same answers as I have and millions of others in the same way. Many people will be at stages of their life where a belief in God is not needed and I totally understand, as my wife is one of them. I never impose my religion upon her or any of my friends, as I believe in respecting all people's beliefs and views just like I would want in return.

People are already saying I have lost the plot and changed, but the way I look at it is that I lost the plot when I was coked up sat in a corner of a pub talking utter nonsense at three in the morning with my jaw swinging!

I do not believe my personality has changed for the worse at all and if it did my wife would totally kick it back into touch. I don't discuss my religious beliefs with anyone unless they ask me, and even then I tell them to find out for themselves by reading and praying for themselves. That's such a simple instruction for some people but so much of a different action to carry out. As a person growing up I always wanted answers to these questions.

Why are we here

Is there life after death

Is there a God and if so why do people suffer?

I am not the most intellectual or well educated man you will ever meet, but I can never understand why a lot of my mates get married or have their children christened in a church and then tell me God and Jesus Christ is a load of rubbish. It beggars belief! But I still love them all and I totally respect their views as I was once the same and I hated people who tried to impose religion on others. Nowadays I just step back and change the subject as if people really want to find the answers they will seek them in time.

I have learnt not to judge anyone and I still mix with my friends who don't agree with my religion but they and I never let it come between our friendships. I am not standing up and saying I have been cured yet from my addictions, as I believe they will hang over my head for many years to come. I still have a long time to go to where I want to be and I know it will take a lifetime of adversity and challenges to breakaway from my past.

Publishing this book will no doubt put me on a pedestal with some people watching me determined to see me fail in my life due to what I have written.   Other people may shake my hand?? I do not know, but for some reason inside I feel this was something I had to do to prove to myself more than anything that I could do something with my life by helping others.

I am not a university graduate in literature, or a recognised author in the worldwide media but I just wanted to try and inspire people from my sort of background that we all have a story that can be told and people want to read about. Every day in my life is still a battle and I face the same challenges as anyone else on this earth, but going to church and learning the principles of the gospel give me strength to achieve things and inspire me.

I have suffered from panic attacks, relapses and bouts of depression, but they have faded less and less over time. Although now when I feel weak, no matter where I am I just pray and ask for strength and get to my feet again. My life continues to change for the better overtime but everyday is a new challenge and I am far from the perfect man. I just wakeup every day thinking to myself "How can I improve?"

I still struggle with smoking and as I speak have had a major relapse with the cigs while on holiday, but when I get home I will start to kick the habit again and get to my feet. One thing I have learnt in the last few months is that it is never too late to change and that nothing is impossible.

If I want proof of that I only have to look back on my life and realise where I was and where I am and what I have already achieved personally. They may be no great achievements to some people but my proudest one is sustaining my family while going through the depths of hell. I exist solely upon this earth for the sacrifices my ancestors gave for me in their lives and I fully intend to forward this to my children.

Football was and still is a major part of my life and I love it immensely even though I was never a great player. I enjoy being a manager and working with young people who want to listen and try to improve each and every game. I have seen it have a huge impact on their social lives as well as improving them as people and this is one of the things that make it addictive to me.

At the moment I am not actively involved as much as I would like to be due to family commitments, but during this time I intend to read as much literature on the role as I can to be the best I can when I return to the game. I think about many of the things I have achieved in my six years of management and it makes me proud. Then I think of what I could have achieved if I had been drug free and this motivates me to become even better qualified and to gain as much knowledge as I possibly can.

This book is based on how the game was a positive and negative ingredient in my life. Football has always been part of me and always will be and that's why I called my story Football for Life, but in the last two years I have learnt that families are forever and that they have to come first...even before football.

CHAPTER 11

ADDICTED

Chapter tunes
Oasis - Cast no shadow
Oasis - Falling down

I'm 37 years of age at the time of me writing this book, and I have had football involved in my life for all those years. If I think about it my Dad was a mad blue in the 70's, so without a shadow of a doubt he would have had the same arguments with my mum that I have had with my wife over football when I was in nappies. So football has always been a part of my family's way of life, so it must have had an effect on the way I was brought up and determined what sort of person I am. It would not have been a huge input but it surely was a significant one. My mum was a red from Wythenshawe and my dad a blue from Salford, anyone in Manchester will tell you in the 70's both areas were quite familiar for being opposite strong city and united strongholds although some may argue.

I always asked my dad what made him be a City fan, as I knew my granddad was a rugby league fan that followed Salford. My granddad lived on Brownfield Close on Ordsall Estate and when I visited him I would sit there for hours, as he would tell me about my dad as a child and the mischief he used to get up to with his cousin's. Most of my dad's cousin's (The Davis's) were all Salford reds and my granddad would say it was typical of my dad to be the "awkward bastard" and he just wanted to be different. My dad would just laugh when I asked him about this and say it was because of the great Joe Mercer team and the way City played football. Often I would get my granddad to repeat it when all the family would be at a family function in Salford and it would lead to an argument between my Uncles Peter and Malcolm, Dad and the others. I would just sit there and laugh with my brother and Peters kids Ian, Alan, the twins (and baby Kimberley).

It would have been much easier for my dad to become a red in Salford and maybe that would have had a different affect on my life totally? Being a City fan I believe has given me something in life I could never have achieved being a red......Faith and Loyalty against all the odds (tongue in cheek!!)

When we use the word addiction we often think straight away of the word drug. Without a shadow of a doubt football has been a drug for millions of us throughout the world, me included. In today's world it is classed as a sort of religion and it's easy to see the comparisons…..

Stadiums full to the brim have replaced churches every week as the meeting points of people looking to get their weekly fix of joy and pain. No matter what team you support at one point or another every football fan will have tasted both. Some maybe more of one than the other, yet we still go back risking pain to feel joy. The fact that we go to the match without knowing the outcome after 90 minutes is what pulls us through the turnstiles (96 minutes in Man Yoo's Case!) Within those 90 minutes absolutely anything is possible and non-more so over the years with my chosen team Manchester City. I would say over 37 years it has been 10 percent joy, 90 percent pain, but I would not change it for the earth.

Manchester City fans have a reputation for being some of the most loyal fans in the world and I often think of why we pulled crowds weekly of over 30,000 a week in Division Three. Why were we different and more loyal than teams like Leeds, Middlesboro, Sheffield Wednesday, and Newcastle United when they were in a similar situation? (Look at the records for attendances although at this moment Leeds are doing the same as we did)

It may have been that during some of those bad times our neighbours from hell, Manchester United were in the most successful period of their history. This might have led to each individual city fan attending having a belief that we can come back from the dead and be as big as them and as successful?? Without a doubt having your closet rival at the top of their game can only be good as it makes you set your standards and goals higher.

The question always plays on my mind, but my own individual belief is that when people are in the face of adversity (ours was MUFC) people pull together and it makes them so much more stronger as a unit. I also believe that each city fan carries an inside belief of "One Day our time will come".

That inside burning in my heart has made me, my brother, dad and all other true city fans carry on supporting our club. A "Belief" that no matter what our brain says negative, our heart still carries positive for some strange reason unbeknown to man. I would expect it is the same for many other fans all over the country, but at this moment in time it just burns a little stronger with us as we have been in the shadow of united for too long. I believe this more than ever after I attended and experienced the Munich Remembrance game at Old Trafford.

As I write this book we have now become tagged the richest football club in the world after a buyout by an Arabian Consortium called ADUG. I have now seen MCFC become the most hated club in the world overnight by the press and media. I have also seen us make an alleged bid of £100 million euros for KAKA! I have also seen a lot of my United mates quaking in their boots but going on the verbal defensive. (Basically being totally negative in a funny sort of way) You could not make it up!

When I was a teenager a lot of my mates played football on a Saturday rather than attend the game watching either City or United. At that time I did not see the big attraction in amateur football and how it could be more addictive participating rather than watching with thousands of other fans.

As I grew older I found out very quickly as I became a football manager what that was, for some people it is the sound the back of a net makes when a ball hits it, for others it is the smell of grass and mud and the passion of 22 players playing in wind, hale or snow purely to win and playing just for the love of the game.

The joy it gave me was the opportunity to build something successful out of nothing. To build a team out of a bunch of individuals who all had different talents and strengths. Any successful football manager from any level of the game will tell you a winning team has to have a mixture of every single ingredient and many of those need to be nurtured and fed.

Now on the eye, or on paper a team might not look like a winning team, but it is if all the jigsaw pieces fit and it comes together on the pitch then you see the big picture. If you want an example of this you only have to look at the Liverpool team of the 70's and 80's. Man United, the treble winning team of in 1999, the European Cup winning teams of Nottingham Forest etc etc. When all the pieces of your jigsaw team come together in a game and you start winning there is no greater feeling or a prouder feeling as a manager. I remember a cup semi-final for my team The Eight Bells. We were 2-1 down against a team called Angel-Riverside from Denton, and we just could not score for love nor money. We hit the bar, had one disallowed, it just was not happening for us at all. Then in the eighty ninth minute we got a corner and one of our players took the worst corner you could think of. It entered the box about six feet off the floor and then all of a sudden "Rennie" came from nowhere and headed the ball in to equalise. I celebrated that goal as much as I would have if Manchester City had won the European Cup. The feeling of relief and joy was something that stays with me to this day and no sport has ever given me that buzz in my life. Myself, the players and about thirty lads on the line went mental and were close to tears. Maybe it was because many of the same players had played in a losing team twelve months earlier and we had all as a unit turned it round with hard work and dedication. We went on to win that match 4-2 in extra time and it was an adrenalin rush like no other purely due to the fact that 99% of our hope had died, but we kept the belief that 1% of what we had left could get us through ...and it did.

Since I have had a family and settled down with a house and wife the opportunity to attend watching football has been limited purely down to the prices of attending. As we all know in today's football climate it is no longer the working mans game, and if I want to take my two kids and wife it would cost me over £75 and that's including parking, food, programme etc. So when I can attend, I now pick my games like most football fans my age. To substitute my addiction to the game I am still heavily involved in amateur football now after five years of managing and I love it.

Like us all I watch a lot of football on television but sat on the settee with your feet up just isn't the same. Once you have been a fan on the terraces you know nothing can replace the aura of thousands of fans on the same level as you. The passion in a stadium passes like an invisible mist from supporter to supporter and creates a spirit that makes the game so addictive. The same can be said about being involved as an amateur manager or player. It's a spirit of togetherness in times of joy and times of pain that you cannot put into words at times. There is not a doubt in my mind that if I would not have had a family or got involved in amateur football I would still be involved in the hooligan scene and using drugs. The reason I was able to walk away was because I substituted that adrenalin rush with being involved as a manager with no risk to other people, myself or my family. This made me fall more in love with the game than ever before. There is no doubt in my mind that I would be dead or in prison if this other door in the world of football would not have been open to me. Football has taught me so many things from man-management skills to curing my drug addiction. Although like anything there has to be a balance as I know many people who have given everything to football and forgotten their families.

I was no different and it is only since I started writing this book that it became apparent to myself. As I was on my way to a training session my six year old daughter stood in front of the door and cried her eyes out telling me that I was always at football. I moved her to the side and told her to get to bed and carried on loading the car up with equipment. Then I just sat in the car and realised how much I had neglected my family. I placed my head against the steering wheel and cried and realised I had missed those six years of my daughter's childhood through football. Cherelle, my oldest daughter was a bit more self-sufficient as she was 21 but I had a grandson Brodie and also a beautiful wife in Amanda and it had dawned on me that I was putting football before them. The more I thought about it the more I thought about the precious weekends I had sacrificed with them for my love of the game. Over the years that had been a mixture of going watching City with the lads to managing teams at the weekend.

It was at that point that I realised football had to come second to my family. Football may be for life but families are forever and eternity. I realised I had a lot of friends in football who had warned me about the dangers of it overtaking your life. I had friends whose wives had left them because of being players and mangers and not being available at the weekend for years. It made me realise that trophies go in the loft, but pictures of the family go on the mantle piece and take pride of place in our homes. This was probably the greatest lesson football taught me and it was that the first team is my home team, and that's my family.

After nearly completing this book it would not be the finished article for me if I did not supply any sort of support for people who are going through cocaine addiction. It will ease my mind and my heart knowing that while I had the opportunity of writing my story I shared things that are still helping me cure my addiction. When I started using Cocaine there wasn't the number of users there are today and I often think about every single person I know who uses it. I know without a doubt in my mind they will go through or have to go through similar experiences.

Friends often ask me how I have stopped, and as I talk to them sadly many tell me they can never see themselves getting off the drug. Well let me tell you, I was once as weak as you and am still no stronger a man than you!

Below you will read how I deal with fighting back and methods I use.

The first thing you have to do is the simplest thing yet the hardest to do. You have to admit you have a problem to yourself first and foremost. In my eyes even if you have just one line a week you have a problem. Ask yourself why you have that line???

Other people will be having it Monday to Friday as well as the weekend, some of you may have it in the daytime or just at the match. Some of you will think you have mastered your use of cocaine and can take it or leave it. Well quite the opposite has occurred, as the drug will show you over time. You will find out it has mastered you by getting you to think that way, and over time it will master your life without you realising it. I found this out myself, as I promised myself when I had my daughter Millie I would stop. I failed miserably despite loving her as much as I do.

This chapter is for people who want help and inspiration. The first thing I can tell you no matter what you think at this point in your life there is a way out and you will do it if you really want to

.

You may have contemplated or even tried ending your life, but the good news is you haven't so forget about it. After admitting to yourself you have a problem you need to share your problem with at least two other people who you love and trust and who are not users. You will find that by doing this it will open up your heart and soul to your problem and this is something I know is the key to it being a success.

The next thing I suggest you do is start attending a Narcotics Anonymous meeting in your local area. N.A meetings are seven days a week, 365 days a year and you will gain strength from hearing other people sharing their experiences. You will also meet some fantastic people and realise you are far from being alone.

For some people it might be a bit weird to be sat in a room with twenty strangers so ask a trusted friend to go with you. N.A will introduce you to prayer and this is something I suggest you do on your own at home in your own privacy.

This will be hard for some people and I fully understand as pride can be your biggest hurdle, but ask yourself what have you got to lose by doing this simple thing? Keep praying every morning and night in your own privacy and ask for strength as if you are talking to your own parents.

Stop drinking and going to the pub with cocaine buddies, you will fail without a shadow of a doubt no matter how strong you think you are.

Replace your pub time with doing something productive like going running or the gym. You could get involved in a local organisation such as a football club or even start your own. The vital thing is you can't stay sat in the house as it will drive you mad. Running with music is a great cure as it gives you time to think alone and create goals in your head. If this happens you must write these goals down and pin them up where you can see them everyday.

Get fit, no matter if it is running, weights or walking. Think of the abuse you have given your body over the years, and have look at yourself in the mirror and ask yourself can you improve? Change your eating habits and another great tip is to drink nothing but water as you will find it will flush all the toxins out of your body. This then will make you less tired and more alert and active in everything you are trying to achieve.

Get out of the house and spend more time with your family and especially your kids if you have any. You will find they love spending time with you and it will become the greatest gift you could ever give them...and guess what it costs nothing. Something as simple as helping them colour a book, or taking them on a bike ride is something that you both will remember when you are older.

One of the greatest days of my life was when I taught my daughter Millie to ride a bike, and then watched as she cycled up a path in Brookdale Park. I think it taught me a bigger lesson than her, as I realised how much she needed me and I needed her. We all as parents are the foundation for our children's futures and it is never too late to make up for lost time even if they are adults. If your children are old enough, think about sharing your problems with them and you will find it will give you strength by making you humble. Another vital thing is to start listening to your kids, even if they are young they will respect you more if you listen, smile and reply with an answer and LOOK into their eyes when talking to them.

A key element of curing my addiction was my wife Mandy. Without doubt it is vital you repair the damage done with friends and family by looking at where you have been going wrong. Look at the influence the drug has had on your life and how it has affected your loved ones and talk about what would have happened if you were clean? Discuss how you are going to change and do not expect your partner to believe you over night. They will want to see the proof is in the pudding and this takes time for them to start believing in you after years of false dawns.

Start to keep a diary and write in it daily, it will help you so much when you read back through it. This will inspire you and lay a greater foundation for you to quit. You may even end up writing a book????

THE MOST IMPORTANT THING

You will never fully quit drugs if you are involved in distributing them or selling them. FACT! I'm no doctor, but stay away from anti-depressant drugs! Sometimes you will may feel that alone you will even think your shadow has left you it gets that bad. The first six months of you quitting will be hellish but it will give you strength like you never imagined. It will make you achieve other things in life you never even dreamed of. If your body becomes sick get to the doctors and ask for help.

NEVER EVER think you have beaten your addiction! This is when you are at your weakest and most vulnerable to start using again. Never give up, even if you have a relapse, learn from your mistake and try not to make the same one again. Replace your cocaine addiction with an addiction for life, because you never know when God will call time on you. Life's like learning to ride a bike, if you keep falling off and ending up on your knee's the only way to succeed is to keep getting back on the bike and you master how to "balance".

As a Christian I have to recommend you search for answers about life by reading the Bible and Book of Mormon and praying. Over time I promise you that you will receive answers no matter if you are an addict, dealer, cripple or even an atheist.

All the above suggestions are impossible to achieve if you are not prepared to strip yourself of pride. If you have faith then God will do this over time. As I finish this book I am now a practising Latter Day Saint and can bear testimony to you that I have tried every which way you can to stop drinking, smoking and drugs, and only now I have started to conquer it. Call it a coincidence and just a sign of someone who's suffering from drug abuse and has lost the plot, but I know I had lost the plot when I was buying a bag of powder and sat in a pub talking total rubbish.

My family do not attend church but respect me and love me for being Simon Cooper. In fact I am quite sure they love me more than the old Simon Cooper who was never in the house.

I have sacrificed football nowadays and put my home life before my football life. This unbelievably has benefited my football life as I am now studying about coaching techniques by reading books and watching DVD's on the subject. I know one day when the time is right for my family I will get involved in football again. When that time comes again I want to be the best educated and qualified manager or coach I can possibly be. In a dream world I would love to work full time in the football industry and I know if I focus I can achieve that as I live in a country and world provided by a god that makes anything possible.

If you would have said to me when I was a ten year old lad bullied at school for my religion that I was going to be an author of a book I would have laughed and said you were mad. Life and football has taught me you get out of life what you put in and that doors are there to be opened.

As Kaka recently said "God has given me a talent and ability but I need to work hard and sweat to achieve my goals"

YOU GOTTA MAKE IT HAPPEN!

CHAPTER 12

THE POWER OF FOOTBALL

Chapter tune
The Farm - All together now

One day last summer I took a ball out of the boot of the car as I was walking in the park with my family. I had a boot full of balls which I had for training the girl's team I was coaching. My daughter Millie was riding her bike and me and my wife talked as we walked around the park. As we walked around I noticed different pockets of people around the park doing different activities. The usual bunch of teenagers playing with a half inflated ball on the grass, old people walking dogs etc. Then I noticed a young man aged about 25 years old with a lad aged about 8 years old. I presumed it was a father and son spending a bit of time together as the dad was talking and the kid was just kicking stones looking uninterested. For some strange reason I kept my eye on them as I walked around the circular cycle path with my family. I was guessing that the young lad did not live with the dad as they looked like they were not communicating very well. I could relate to this as my parents split up at a young age and I was exactly the same. One second lap round the cycle track for some strange reason I felt the urge to give the young lad the ball. "Here mate you can have this ball, my daughters more interested in riding her bike" The young lad and his dad gave me a smile and I carried on walking as my wife Mandy was calling me stupid as I was always giving things away. After a minute I turned around to see the father and the son both smiling and laughing as they were trying to tackle each other to gain the possession of the ball. I looked at Mandy and just grinned "Look how powerful that ball has just become, it's just made two people happy who were sad exactly two minutes ago" The way that £5 football transformed the emotions of that father and son will stay with me for life as it has proved to me how powerful just a simple thing like a football can become.

The following article is by a world class reporter called Malcolm Doney and it's the note I want to finish the book on so hopefully we can all feed off his words and let them stay with us every time we watch the game whether its on a street, a grass pitch or a premier league football pitch.

Thanks to Malcolm Doney of http://www.developments.org.uk

Can the power of football be harnessed for good?

The TV commercial is grainy and cool – shot in muted, almost sepia tones over a Latin music track. Millionaire football stars Ronaldo and Zinedine Zidane languidly display their awesome ball skills in an empty auditorium, their shoes squeaking on the floor boards. It is captioned "the most beautiful soccer moves". You wait for the logo of some global sports or soft drinks brand but it fails to appear. Instead, the two stop playing, pick up a ball each and thrust a hand towards the camera. Ronaldo tells us: "For us, a helping hand is the best hand of all." A voice-over says, "Together let's reach the world's goal of halving poverty by 2015". Ronaldo and Zidane are acting in their roles as goodwill ambassadors for the United Nations Development Programme.

On a dirt pitch in the dwindling light, a teenage goalkeeper stands tense between the twigs that mark his goal, trying to make out the ball as the outfield players seek a winning goal in Kibera, a Nairobi slum. The referee blows his whistle and 15 year old Kenny Arinda, the goalie, gathers both teams on the touchline. But there is no post-match analysis. Instead, Kenny, himself an AIDS orphan, talks to the boys frankly, amid nudges and laughter, about safe sex and the prevention of HIV. As a volunteer for the Kibera Community Self Help Programme (KICOSHEP), a UNICEF-supported community project, he organises these matches in order to raise awareness about Aids and sexual health.

In Tanzania, a weary British football team plays the last match of a grueling 15-country African tour which started in Senegal. Fourteen of the 20-man squad have tested positive for malaria, and diarrhea is rife among the group. During the last part of the tour it has been hard to select a fit team even for seven-a-side. These volunteers have spent their own money to join TackleAfrica, the brainchild of advertising exec Ben Maitland, which is sponsored by Christian Aid and Concern. The arrival of Europeans in a town or village for a match against the local side draws a healthy crowd and is the occasion for a flurry of activity organised by Christian Aid or Concern's local partners to raise awareness of HIV/AIDS. Which is why they came here in the first place.

Each of these examples, in their own way, is an attempt to harness the power of football for the benefit of humanity because powerful the game certainly is. When FIFA, soccer's world governing body, last did a head count (in 2000) it estimated that over 240 million people regularly played football around the globe, including 20 million women. Add children to that number, plus anyone who joins in an occasional kick about, and then include those whose fitness, age or ineptitude allow them only to enthuse (and opine) – and the reach of football is vast. Obvious when you think about it – after all, you only need a patch of ground, a ball of some description and a group of people who want a game. A beach, a street, a building site, a corridor – any become a field of dreams. Ironically, football's huge popularity among the poor means that the game at the top of the professional level has become very rich indeed. Slowly too slowly for some – football is examining its own conscience.

"As world football's supreme body, FIFA is responding openly to its social duty as an organisation of international status and renown." said Sepp Blatter FIFA President, "It also acknowledges the prominent role of sport, and especially football, as a vehicle for delivering clear and firm messages to eradicate the huge blights undermining society around the world."

In recent years FIFA has established links with UNICEF, WHO, ILO and adopted SOS Children's Villages as its semi-official charity. FIFA provides $250,000 to each of its nation members for football infrastructure but provides grants, often for more social-oriented initiatives, through its international "Goal Programme". The 2002 World Cup in Korea and Japan was dedicated to children under the banner of "Say Yes for Children" – the first time a FIFA World Cup has been dedicated to a humanitarian cause. FIFA intends to pursue its alliance with UNICEF and "will continue to work with other humanitarian organisations that strive to improve the lot of children in our world. Because when it comes to the kids, football is a force for change unlike any other." Quite so.

A pioneer of developing links between football and the cause of children has been Liberian-born Chelsea and AC Milan star George Weah. In 1994, the year before he was named FIFA's World Player of the Year, he founded a children's team in Monrovia, the Junior Professionals, whose membership requirement was attendance at school. In 1997 he became a UNICEF goodwill ambassador. More recently he has been using his influence to help child soldiers in his home country to return to normality. "War is over" he told crowds in the New Year, adding that childen "should disarm and get back to school". Weah, described as the "African Pride" by Nelson Mandela for his humanitarian work, believes football can play an important unifying role: "Sports are important to the peace process. Through games like football we can do something to heal the minds of children."

Perhaps it can work for adults too. England's Football Association thinks so, and since 2000 has established an International Relations programme principally to promote soccer, but also in the hope of "using the power of football to build a better future". Last year, the FA sent Jonathan Day, Football Development Officer for East Riding County, on a fact-finding visit to Bosnia and Serbia to assess a football-based initiative run by humanitarian organisation Open Fun Football.

"Seeing the effects of a war at first hand was frightening," he recalled. "But I also found that no matter what happens people can still learn to live together and make friendships."

Out on the pitch were Serbs, Croats, Bosnians, Muslims – people who were shooting at one another in the streets five years before, now playing for each other. "I am convinced that I witnessed the true power of football in the Balkans. Played in the right spirit, football can have an unbelievable influence."

Perhaps what football does best is to help restore a sense of normality to a traumatized community – an outlet for energy and passion where winning and losing is no longer ultimately a question of life or death. Former British Army Major Michael Moriarty is the FA's representative on the Football Task Force in Afghanistan, also supported by the Foreign & Commonwealth Office and the British Council. The task force grew out of the historic football match played between a team made up of the nations from the coalition forces of the International Security Assistance Force and players drawn from four Kabul teams. The match was played in front of an enthusiastic crowd of 30,000 in the stadium formerly used by the Taliban for public executions and torture. Yes, it was a PR exercise, but also symbolic of an intention to rebuild a sporting culture that had been suppressed for many years. Moriarty believes "football has a huge part to play in reviving Afghanistan after all the bloodshed and violence."

Similar moves are afoot in Iraq, with attempts being made to re-establish a football federation, and Care International's footie4Iraq programme helping providing kit and equipment at grassroots level. The Iraqi football team, once the plaything of Uday Hussein – who tortured players who "failed" – visits the UK in May.

Other symbolic initiatives such as Truce International, founded by England football coach Sven-Gorn Eriksson and his partner Nancy Dell'Olio, are also underway. Inspired by the occasion, on Boxing Day 1914, when British and German soldiers left their opposing trenches to kick a ball about, Truce aims to act as a fundraising focus for a range of peace-building football programmes. Their prime ambition is to create a dedicated national day of youth-related football events or, as board member John Carmichael puts it to "campaign to stop the world fighting for a day to play football".

In fact there is a bewildering number of ideas and programmes around, some more coherent than others, many with undeniable merit – notably the "Dreams & Teams" initiative of the British Council which helps young people in poor countries develop leadership skills by setting up their own sports festivals. But mostly, governments and agencies are playing a game of catch up. It was only in 2002, for example, that the UN inter-agency task force on sport for development and peace was set up, "to encourage a more coherent approach to the use of sport-related initiatives in the pursuit of United Nations development goals". Its first major report, a year later, concluded that "the United Nations has only scratched the surface of possibilities for integrating physical activity, recreation and sports activities into development programming". It said there was an over reliance on sporting stars as ambassadors and there is now a need "to step beyond celebrity and elite sports in ways that convert spectators into participants". It continued: "The aim of United Nations activities involving sport is not the creation of new sporting champions and the development of sport but rather the use of sport in broader development and peace-building activities."

The report sets an ambitious and timely agenda. "Sport is yet to be mainstreamed into the development agenda or the United Nations system. In general, sports initiatives to date have been ad hoc, informal, and isolated. The time is ripe to develop a coherent and systematic strategy for increasing the use of sport within the United Nations." For sport read football. It is the beautiful game, the world game. Perhaps, given extra time, it could save lives.

FIFA/ United Nations…….. The Balls in your half………

CHAPTER 13

"STOPPAGE TIME"

Like football this book has had to have some stoppage time as my soul tells me that 180 pages is not enough and I feel I can just put a little more into this.   At the time of me writing this I am late signing the book off, and after studying it my wife and I noticed spelling mistakes and a few badly worded paragraphs.

As I may have mentioned before in the book my spelling is terrible and my timing of paragraphs is not the best to say the least. I have never been the best at literature and people constantly pull me up on the way I pronounce words and my interpretation of words. I may be slightly dyslexic I do not know but I pray that you get the message of my story and why I wrote it.

In football stoppage time can be the most crucial time in a game as both teams mentally can believe the game is over. Pride comes into their heads and they become weak as they believe the job is complete. It is only the great teams that have mastered that this is the prime time to achieve a result in a match that should be 90 minutes. They step up their game as they are taught that when a team thinks they have won with time still on the clock then they are at their most vulnerable. I hope you allow me to get my winner in by getting my message across in stoppage time with this final chapter.

My life has changed a lot since I started writing and it has made me have a real look at myself and my surroundings. As I write this I am trying to arrange and organise the first football trip ever to the city of Tamale in Ghana by an English amateur football team. My friend Peter K Amoabil had a picture of his team in their full kit with no socks or boots on in Ghana and I just felt the need to do something to improve their lives. The support I have received is unreal and it has made me realise there are a lot of good people in this world and it is just a matter of finding them and asking for help.

I have realised after reading this book that at times in my life I have thought I have had a bad deal with my family life and my upbringing as a child. After writing this book and looking at other peoples lives I now know that I have had an easy life compared to a large population of this world and this country. It has made me humble and more determined to give a bit back to my community and the world instead of looking to see how much I can take from it.

I have totally walked away from being a plumber as I don't feel anymore it's the job I want to do in my life. Instead I have got a job helping people rebuild their lives by getting employment and stability. Many of these people have little or a poor education, many are ex-convicts, criminals, immigrants, drug addicts or disabled people. The most important thing to me is that they are all human beings who need a little help. The money is nowhere near what I could earn as a plumber, but at this stage in my life I don't feel attracted as much to money as I use to be.

I feel I can relate to these people who need a little help as it was once me who needed help. That day a friend I once ignored and turned my back on never gave up on me and knocked on my door, so I feel it's my duty to do what he did to me. Never give up on people!

The thing with change is that people fear change in anything, especially if that change is too quick to comprehend. Change installs fear into people and its one lesson we all have to learn no matter what age we are or where we are from. At this moment in time this country has a problem with immigration which is causing tension. The reason it is causing tension is because the population is scared of the unknown and the future.

It was exactly the same with the Jamaican and Indian immigration in the 1950's and 1960's. These people did not look the same or dress the same so they were despised by many British citizens and branded as aliens. Before the Jamaicans and Indians it was the Irish immigrant workers who were despised and hated and abused. (my Grandfather being one)

Nowadays it is the Asians, Somalians, Africans and basically anyone who does not look or dress British.

I want you to forget the colour of people's skin, their religion, or their dress for just five minutes. I want you to imagine a totally white, yellow, brown or black world and think about what it would be like. Perfect you may say….. well you need to think deeper.

The next problem would be what colour eyes you have or what colour hair you have. It may even come down to if you are fat, thin, tall or small. It would affect us all and our families exactly the same as it does now.

People need to open their minds and their hearts to change as it is happening every second, every hour and every day we live on this earth. Hate is not the solution on anyone's part and will solve nothing as many wars have shown us. We need to strip ourselves of pride and put our barriers down and listen and communicate more as a world. Sport can do this with everyone and I can prove this to you with one short story.

THE POWER OF SPORT

What would you do?....you make the choice. Don't look for a punch line, there isn't one. Read it anyway. My question is would you have made the same choice?

At a fundraising dinner for a school that serves children with learning disabilities, the father of one of the students delivered a speech that would never be forgotten by all who attended.

After extolling the school and its dedicated staff, he offered a question:

'When not interfered with by outside influences, everything nature does is done with perfection. Yet my son, Shay, cannot learn things as other children

do. He cannot understand things as other children do.

"Where is the natural order of things in my son?"'

The audience was stilled by the query. The father continued. 'I believe that when a child like Shay, who was mentally and physically disabled comes into the world, an opportunity to realise true human nature presents itself, and it comes in the way other people treat that child.'

Then he told the following story:

Shay and I had walked past a park where some boys Shay knew were playing baseball. Shay asked, 'Do you think they'll let me play?' I knew that most of the boys would not want someone like Shay on their team, but as a father I also understood that if my son were allowed to play, it would give him a much-needed sense of belonging and some confidence to be accepted by others in spite of his handicaps. I approached one of the boys on the field and asked (not expecting much) if Shay could play. The boy looked around for guidance and said, 'We're losing by six runs and the game is in the eighth inning. I guess he can be on our team and we'll try to put him in to bat in the ninth inning.'

Shay struggled over to the team's bench and, with a broad smile, put on a team shirt. I watched with a small tear in my eye and warmth in my heart. The boys saw my joy at my son being accepted. In the bottom of the eighth inning

Shay's team scored a few runs but was still behind by three. In the top of the ninth inning Shay put on a glove and played in the right field. Even though no hits came his way, he was obviously ecstatic just to be in the game and on the field, grinning from ear to ear as I waved to him from the stands. In the bottom of the ninth inning, Shay's team scored again. Now, with two outs and the bases loaded, the potential winning run was on base and Shay was scheduled to be next at bat. At this juncture, do they let Shay bat and give away their chance to win the game? Surprisingly, Shay was given the bat.

Everyone knew that a hit was all but impossible because Shay didn't even know how to hold the bat properly, much less connect with the ball. However, as Shay stepped up to the plate, the pitcher, recognising that the other team was putting winning aside for this moment in Shay's life, moved in a few steps to lob the ball in softly so Shay could at least make contact. The first pitch came and Shay swung clumsily and missed. The pitcher again took a few steps forward to toss the ball softly towards Shay. As the pitch came in, Shay swung at the ball and hit a slow ground ball right back to the pitcher.

The game would now be over. The pitcher picked up the soft grounder and could have easily thrown the ball to the first baseman. Shay would have been out and that would have been the end of the game. Instead, the pitcher threw the ball right over the first baseman's head, out of reach of all team mates.

Everyone from the stands and both teams started yelling, 'Shay, run to first! Run to first!' Never in his life had Shay ever run that far, but he made it to first base. He scampered down the baseline, wide-eyed and startled. Everyone yelled, 'Run to second, run to second!' Catching his breath, Shay awkwardly ran towards second, gleaming and struggling to make it to the base. By the time Shay rounded towards second base, the right fielder had the ball, the smallest guy on the team who now had his first chance to be the hero for his team.

He could have thrown the ball to the second baseman for the tag, but he understood the pitcher's intentions so he too, intentionally threw the ball high and far over the third-baseman's head. Shay ran toward third base deliriously, as the runners ahead of him circled the bases toward home. All were screaming, 'Shay, Shay, Shay, all the Way Shay' Shay reached third base because the opposing shortstop ran to help him by turning him in the direction of third base, and shouted, 'Run to third! Shay, run to third!' As Shay rounded third, the boys from both teams, and the spectators, were on their feet screaming, 'Shay, run home! Run home! 'Shay ran to home, stepped on the plate, and was cheered as the hero who hit the grand slam and won the game for his team.

'That day', said the father softly with tears now rolling down his face, 'the boys from both teams helped bring a piece of true love and humanity into this world'.

Shay didn't make it to another summer. He died that winter, having never forgotten being the hero and making me so happy, and coming home and seeing his Mother tearfully embrace her little hero of the day!

A wise man once said every society is judged by how it treats it's least fortunate amongst them.

I do not know the colour of the skin of any of the players involved in that game. Nor do I know what countries their families descend from or what clothes they wear or what class of society they live in. I do not know what language any of them spoke of the colour of their hair or if they were fat or thin tall or small.

What I do know however is that they were all human and all had hearts and a love of sport. I also know that every player and person who witnessed that game on that pitch that day could not have ever dreamed of the positive ripple effect that game could have had on people like me and you.

We can all have that same affect on the world by simply living our daily lives with a smile and by being more humble and understanding of other people who may look different on the outside, but are exactly the same as you and me on the inside.

No matter what your religion, colour, language, nationality, football team, background or life we are all part of the same family as we are all sons and daughters of God and it is something we need to REMEMBER.

ACKNOWLEDGMENTS

First and foremost I'd like to thank my family for putting up with me even though at times I have put them through hell, Mandy, Cherelle, Millie, Ryan, Brodie. My Mum, Dad, Ann, Katie, Nick, Louis, Beth, and all my nephews and nieces.

Anthony Rowan, Mike Chetcuti, Craig Reed and Aki, Clive and OB for never giving up on life or me, by inspiring me to keep on getting up off the floor to fight another day.

Everyone involved in Amateur Football in Manchester who has given me an education and opportunity of being involved in football. Bruno, Brendan Edge, Johnny Ham, Terry Pickup, Moxy, Leo, Neil, Billy Grogan, Pat Dillon, Alan McCuen, Wayne Kenndy, Wayne Joynes, Steve B and Red Star F.C to name but a few.

Big thanks to every individual player who has played for or played against one of my teams. Including Derbo, Bowler, Houghton, Ratty, Edgy, Gavo, Robbie, Shaunno, Kyle Wallwork, Boardy, Matt Grandon, Smell, Platty, Wolfy, Armie, Starkie, Gally, Teaser, Limo, Doddy, Mike Taylor, Mark Elliot, Tony N, The Grey Horse and everybody at Moston Villa and The Railway in Newton Heath and last but not least Quinny at the Guido.

Colin Little and Aran Burns and all the Wythenshawe lads for being true loyal friends and making me smile and laugh throughout my life.

Codge, Rozzi Baz and all the Bluewatch team (www.bluewatchmcfc. co.uk)

All the lads at the match who I grew up with watching City and I shall never ever forget and truly love like brothers:

Tate brothers, Koosh, Masters, Blacky, John From Chad, Eddy Dolan, Salford John, Johnny Dale, The Set Up 6, Colin and Paul Coleman, Chris Harrop, Pat G, Barry and Haydyn Foy, Bootsy and Scott, Simmo, Aki, Lee Pickup, Colin Arthur, Shawey, Simon The Tarmac, Fairy, Kells, Chris F, Botty, The Prestwich Firm, Ben, Sean, Trav, Noodles, Stu, Dean, The Wally and Engine families, The Israel Family, Frankie, Big K, Leon x 2, Paddy, Housey, Foggy, Bangers, Danials, Scooby, Rodney, Carl S, Brad Doyle, Tranter, Dryer, Walshy, Peter Wright, Sykesy, Sadman, Scouse, Dave the Rave, Cliff from Wythenshawe, Watty, Scully, Franny Charles, Balk, Eddie and Tony W, Kinnock, Julian and all the ticket tout firm. Warren, Sheane, Kieron R, Dogs, The Twins, Big Rod, Slash, Dom, Wacker, Basher, Barry, Jacko, Big Gav, Peter Furnival, Paul from Monton and all the Salford blues, Chrisy James, Peter Sahr, Paul Rothwell, Craig Rowlands, Jez, Terry, Derbo, Brains, Stretch, Ste, Val, Little Murphy, Phil the DJ, Roy Foulkes, Anthony Plythian and all the Miles Platting and Ancoats Blues, Pat B, Jub, Mickey Carr, Ruso, Jamie R, Colin Jones, Johnny Gunnings, Dennis, Smythes, Foreshaw and all the Parkside lads, Lumby and the Moston blues.

R.I.P. Gary Rogers

R.I.P. Darren Price

R.I.P. Mikey Williams

R.I.P. Billy Grogan

R.I.P. Jason Martin

I would need two pages to write all your names of the rest of you, but you all know who you are.

To all the Failsworth Reds for putting up with me:

Gav, Wayne and Danny Pinder, Johnny Egan, Presi, Tony Cannon, Nick Duff, Albert, Twiggy, Billy Jordan, Tony Jordan, Ravo, Scully, Kenny Williams etc etc. Many of you are like brothers to me and you know who you are.

To all the Failsworth blues Lofty, Terry Qualters, Tipler, Tony Ellis, Crossa, Maxine, Tapper, Backhouse, Kelly's Hero's, Moggy, Jimbo, again too many to name.

ADUG for making every Manchester City fans dreams reality. Gary Cook for believing in the fans by listening.

Bobby Charlton for being one of the most humble and nicest people I have ever met.

Matt Brown, Young Bernie Bolger, Tony Murray, Jay Martin, Crazy Moynie, Joe Rowan, Ellis, Davo, The Muzz brothers, Tommy Macela and sons, and The 8 Bells Demolition Squad. Every pupil I went to school with at Failsworth and Mather Street School from 1974 to 1988.

All the people of Failsworth, Newton Heath, Moston , Miles Platting, Ancoats, Beswick, Clayton, Droylsden, Blackley, Hollinwood, Chadderton........I love you all dearly as your humour makes me proud to be a mancunian.

Every person that I have worked with or have been brave enough to ever employ me and give me an opportunity of working. Jim Wibberley, Ian Hunt, Paul Monaghan, Steve Brooks, Tom Harkin, Chris O'Connor John Gregory, Jay Clark, Ray Clarke, Derek Oliver, Johnny Brierley, Woody, Alan, Mellorman, Craig B and Brothers, Peter Hemlin to name but a few.

All the lads in Australia, Nev Taylor, Heath, Maffu, Jacko, Jordan, Barkle, Palmer and the Wolfgramme and Mafoa Family. I miss you all dearly.

Jason Denny From Los Angeles

Every person who has ever shared at an N.A. meeting as you all inspire me.

The Mayall Family, The Ashworth Family, The Gore Family, The Morris Family, The Beresford Family, The Carruthers family, My cousins and Aunt Eileen in America, Bishop and family. Thomas S. Monson, Spencer W. Kimball.

A huge thank you to my Gran Eunice for pulling me out of trouble for twenty years, and my greatest friend who has now passed away, my Grandad Harry. To my Gran Nell and Grandad Liam, I miss you very much and think of you a lot. All my Aunts and Uncles and Cousins, Laura and Mike, Camilla, Nathan etc.

To Michelle Price (and Zoe) for being the big sister my wife and me never had. Also to say thanks to my departed friends Gary Rogers, Stephen Hurst and Darren Price who lost their lives so young. I know I will see you again and you all live on in my heart.

To Johnny Cash, Noel and Liam Gallagher for writing fantastic lyrics that inspired me and cleansed my mind to write this book it's a fine line between Genius and Insanity)

Thank you to everyone who makes me laugh, especially:

Stafford, Bernie, Gizmo, Coonack, Nico, Backhouse, Whitey, Newton, Darren Beswick and the Trickster himself Anthony Atkinson.

JJ Connolly the author of Layer Cake for coming in my house and telling me his amazing story and giving me belief.

And last but not least thanks to God and his only begotten son, the Lord and Saviour Jesus Christ for giving me the opportunity of baptism and repentance so I can start again and repair the damage I have done by serving his church upon this earth. (Hopefully through football)

Thy Will Be Done.

Without their inspiration this book would never have been completed.

Peace and Love Simon Cooper.

A FEW TIPS ON BEING A GOOD AMATEUR MANAGER.

A successful soccer team is often a stable team. Here is a guide to how to make a team by laying these 7 foundations

1. Get to know your players

You may have a very clear idea of the particular soccer qualities that a new player possesses, but what do you know beyond that? By gaining a greater understanding of your players as individuals you can help improve your ability to integrate and motivate them.

Players care about what you know when they know that you care about them. Get them to complete a player information sheet that asks them about all areas of their lives.

Encourage the players to be as honest as they can. Emphasise that it helps build effective teams and encourages clear communication. Most importantly, once you have collected this information – use it!

By making the effort to get to know the player, and not just for their soccer can pay dividends when trying to understand their wider motivations. The process of asking is a classic motivational tool for the player – it shows you care.

2. Make use of your senior players

Ask them for their opinions on how best to integrate new players, as well as feedback on how the new players are settling in.

Pair up new players with experienced team members. This will help the new players feel less like outsiders and will help them quickly pick up the values and behaviours expected of and by the squad.

3. Avoid cliques

Cliques are groups of players who stick together. Avoid cliques by splitting up players to work in different groups or on different teams in training. If you have the opportunity, for example on tour, varies whom the players room or eat with.

Team discussions (see below) can also promote positive relationships within the team and make players aware of the damage cliques can cause. Whilst it is inevitable that players will spend more time with some team-mates than others, cliques tend to be disruptive and are exclusive.

4. Team meetings

Spend time before or after training with team meetings. New players can be given the opportunity to work with other players in small groups (thus continuing the work of avoiding cliques), can be given the responsibility of feeding back to the whole squad, or their views on a particular issue, for example match strategy, can be invited.

To help the new player the coach can let them know in advance, or even discuss on a one-to-one basis, what they will be required to comment on. This gives the player time to prepare and approach the meeting with more confidence. In this way the new player can begin to feel a part of the squad as his views are shown to be valued.

5. Roles and responsibilities

Make sure a player understands (and accepts) his role within the team and any responsibilities that go with it. Clarify any other expectations concerning for example, behaviour, match day dress, and so on.

All players hate being criticised for doing (or not doing) something they did not know about in the first place! As with all the other points, this is about maintaining clear and open communication.

One useful exercise for clarifying responsibilities is to list all the responsibilities a player has in a specific position whilst asking them to do the same. Any discrepancies can then be clarified, and the role can be understood and agreed to by the player.

6. Honesty, Belief and Family.

The most vital aspect I believe in being a manager is being a good example away from football as well as on the coaching pitch. If this means changing your lifestyle then do it as you will find it will make you a better person if you are seeking to become a winner. Practise what you preach and never lie to your staff and especially yourself.

The key to being a great football manager is respecting your family and the families of the players. If you can master how to combine the two to your advantage you will have a dream team.

7.Preparation and Education

Get as much education on management and football as you can. Your brain is a sponge and if you can't afford to do the FA coaching badges join a library and read every night, watch coaching films which are available for free on Youtube.

Give your players the best equipment you can but make sure that they commit to raising the money so this is possible. You will find that they respect the equipment and kit more if they have had to work hard for it.

Finally prepare every training session you do by writing it down on paper and revise it. If you are training for 36 weeks in a year then do a structure of training sessions and write down and set goals.

The key to being successful in life is what foundation your structure is built on for you to succeed. That is how you rise or fall in your quest to success in anything whether it is family, football or work.

ACKNOWLEDGEMENTS

First and foremost my family for putting up with me even though at times I have put them threw hell. Mandy, Cherelle, Milly, Ryan, Brody. My Mum, Dad, Ann, Katie, Nick, Louis, Beth, and all my nephews and nieces.

Anthony Rowan, Mike Chetcuti, Craig Reed and Aki, Clive and OB for never giving up on life or me, by inspiring me to keep on getting up off the floor to fight another day.

JJ Connolly the author of Layer Cake for coming in my house and telling me his amazing story and giving me belief.

Manchester City Football Club

Everyone involved in Amateur Football in Manchester who has given me an education and opportunity of being involved in football. Bruno, Brenden Edge, Johnny Ham, Terry Pickup, Moxy, Leo , Neil, Billy Grogan, Pat Dillon, Alan McCuen, Wayne Kenndy, Wayne Joynes, Steve B and Red Star F.C. to name but a few.

Big thanks to every individual player who has played for or played against one of my teams. Including Derbo, Bowler, Houghton, Ratty, Edgy, Gavo, Robbie, Shaunno, Kyle Wallwork, Boardy, Matt Grandon, Smell, Platty, Wolfy, Armie, Starkie, Gally, Teaser, Limo, Doddy, Mike Taylor, Mark Elliot, Tony N, The Grey Horse and everybody at Moston Villa and The Railway in Newton Heath and last but not least Quinny at the Guido.

Colin Little and Aran Burns and all the Wythenshaw lads for being true loyal friends and making me smile and laugh threw out my life.

All the lads at the match who I grew up with watching City and I shall never ever forget and truly love like brothers:

 Tate brothers, Koosh, Masters, Blacky, John From Chad,Jonah, Crozza, Eddy Dolan, Salford John, Johnny Dale, The Set Up 6, Colin and Paul Coleman, Chris Harrop, Pat G, Barry and Haydyn Foy, Bootsy and Scott, Simmo, Aki, Lee Pickup, Colin Arthur, Shawey, Simon The Tarmac, Fairy, Kells, Chris F, Botty, The Prestwich Firm, Ben, Sean, Trav, Noodles, Stu, Dean, The Wally and Engine families, The Israel Family, Frankie, Big K, Leonx2, Paddy, Housey, Foggy, Bangers, Danials, Scooby, Rodney, Carl S, Brad Doyle, Tranter, Dryer, Walshy, Peter Wright, Sykesy, Sadman, Scouse, Dave the Rave, Dave Hazlewood and all his family, Cliff from Wythenshawe, Watty, Scully, Franny Charles, Balk, Eddie and Tony W, Kinnock, Julian and all the ticket tout firm.

Warren, Sheane, Kieron R, Dogs, The Twins, Big rod, Slash, Dom, Wacker, Basher, Barry, Jacko, Big Gav, Peter Furnival, Paul from Monton and all the Salford blues, Chrisy James, Peter Sahr, Paul Rothwell, Craig Rowlands, Jez, Terry, Derbo, Brains, Stretch, Ste, Val, Little Murphy, Phil the DJ, Roy Foulkes, Anthony Plythian and all the Miles Platting and Ancoats Blues, Pat B, Jub, Mickey Carr, Ruso, Jaimie R, Colin Jones, Johnny Gunnings, Dennis, Smythes, Foreshaw and all the Parkside lads, Lumby and the Moston blues.

R.I.P. Gary Rogers

R.I.P. Darren Price

R.I.P. Mikey Williams

R.I.P. Billy Grogan

R.I.P. Jason Martin

I would need 2 pages to write all your names of the rest of you, but you know who you are.

To all the Failsworth Reds for putting up with me:

Gav, Wayne and Danny Pinder, Johnny Egan, Presi, Tony Cannon, Nick Duff, Albert, Twiggy, Billy Jordan, Tony Jordan, Ravo, Scully, Kenny Williams, Stafford etc etc. Many of you are like brothers to me and you know who you are.

To all the Failsworth Blues Lofty, Terry Qualters, Tipler, Tony Ellis, Webby, Maxine, Tapper, Backhouse, Kelly's Hero's, Moggy, Jimbo, again too many to name.

ADUG for making every Manchester City fans dreams reality. Gary Cook for believing in the fans by listening.

Bobby Charlton for being one of the most humble and nicest people I have ever met.

Matt Brown, Bernie Bolger, Sniper, Tony Murray, Crazy Moynie, Joe Rowan, Ellis, Davo, Chris Murray, Tommy Macela and sons, and The 8 Bells Demolition Squad. Every pupil I went to school with at Failsworth and Mather Street School from 1974 to 1986.

All the people of Failsworth, Newton Heath, Moston , Miles Platting, Ancoats, Beswick, Clayton, Droylsden, Blakley, Hollinwood, Chadderton........I love you all dearly as your humor makes me proud to be a mancunian.

Every person that I have worked with or have been brave enough to ever employ me and give me an opportunity of working. Jim Wibberley, Ian Hunt, Paul Monaghan, Steve Brooks, Tom Harkin, Chris O'Connor John Gregory, Jay Clark, Ray Clarke, Derek Oliver, Johnny Brierley, Woody, Alan, Mellorman, Craig B and Brothers, Peter Hemilin to name but a few.

All the lads in Australia, Nev Taylor, Heath, Maffu, Jacko, Jordan, Barkle, Palmer and the Wolfgramme and Mafoa Family. I miss you all dearly.

Jason Denny From Los Angeles

Every person who has ever shared at an N.A. meeting as you all inspire me.

The Mayall Family, The Ashworth Family, The Gore Family, The Morris Family, The Beresford Family, The Carruthers family, My cousins and Aunt Eileen in America, Bishop and family. Thomas S. Monson, Spencer W. Kimball.

A huge thank you to my Gran Eunice for pulling me out of trouble for 20 years, and my greatest friend who has now passed away my Grandad Harry.

To my Gran Nell and Grandad Liam, I miss you very much and think of you a lot. All my Aunts and Uncles and Cousins...Laura and Mike, Camilla, Nathan etc.

To Michelle Price (and Zoe) for being the big sister my wife and me never had. Also to say thanks to my departed friends Gary Rogers, Stephen Hurst and Darren Price who lost their lives so young. I know I will see you again and you all live on in my heart.

To Johnny Cash, Noel and Liam Gallagher, Lilly Allen for writing fantastic lyrics that inspired me and cleansed my mind to write this book.(it's a fine line between Genius and Insanity)

Thank you to everyone who makes me laugh, especially:

Stafford, Bernie, Gizmo, Coonack, Nico, Backhouse, Whitey, Newton, Darren Beswick and the Trickster himself Anthony Atkinson.

And last but not least thanks to God and his only begotten son, the Lord and Savior Jesus Christ for giving me the opportunity of baptism and repentance so I can start again and repair the damage I have done by serving his church upon this earth. (Hopefully threw football)

Without their inspiration this book would never have been completed.

Love Simon Cooper.

The 8 Bells winning team that beat the previously unbeaten White Horse 4-1...
Impossible is nothing!

Anthony Rowan. The Man City Fans legend who is a inspiration to many of his friends and family. Who now fights a daily battle against M.S. but is still Manchester City mad.

Blootoof AKA Codge's two nephews outside the Eastlands Stadium.

Brendan Edge and Moston Villa F.C.

Bruno and the Crown and Cushion Team.

Some of the city lads at one of the charity events we organised.

Dennis, Tom, Geoff and the Royal Antwerp Casuals whose second team is Manchester City
of course.

"The Failsworth Town" A team i ran with lads from Failsworth,Newton Heath, Miles Platting and Ancoats. Spot the United fans?

The last city trip I organized away to Middlesboro away in 2006/07. Two coaches full of friends for life.

Breinigsville, PA USA
31 January 2010
231657BV00001B/37/P